NORTHERN
FLIGHTS

NORTHERN
FLIGHTS

GERRY BRUDER

PRUETT **P** PUBLISHING COMPANY
Boulder, Colorado

Printed in the United States of America

First Edition
1 2 3 4 5 6 7 8 9

Library of Congress Cataloging-in-Publication Data

Bruder, Gerry, 1944-
    Northern flights / Gerry Bruder.
        p.   cm.
    ISBN 0-87108-739-1 (pbk.)
    1. Bruder, Gerry, 1944-   .   2. Air pilots–Alaska–Biography.
I. Title.
TL540.B7447A3 1988
629.13'092'4–dc19
[B]   88-19200
                                                                            CIP

Cover woodcut by Patty Miller.
Book and cover design by Jody Chapel, Cover to Cover Design

To southeastern Alaska's professional floatplane pilots—
past, present, and future.

CONTENTS

Southeastern Alaska

Adams Inlet
Lynn Canal
Muir Inlet
Endicott River
Juneau Ice Cap
Taku River
Elfin Cove
Juneau
Taku Inlet
Hoonah
Tenakee
Chichagof Is
Angoon
Gambier Bay
Chaik Bay
Sitka
Kuiu Is
Kake
Baranof Is
Petersburg
Labouchere Bay
Wrangell
Brownson Is
Sumner Strait
Behm Canal
Kosciusko Is
Bell Is
Revillagigedo Is
Tuxekan Is
Hyder
Heceta Is
Coffman Cove
Meyers Chuck
Steamboat Bay
Cleveland Peninsula
Noyes Is
Klawock
Harris River
Kasaan Peninsula
Trocadero Bay
Craig
Hollis
Twelve-Mile Arm
Ketchikan
Big Goat Lake
Hydaburg
Tongass Narrows
Hetta Inlet
Metlakatla
Annette Is
Misty Fjords National Mon
Prince of Wales Is
Cholmondeley Sound

PREFACE

Some people I meet in the Lower Forty-eight states chuckle when I tell them I'm a bush pilot in Alaska. Believing that the bush pilot long ago faded into the sunset, they assume I'm teasing them. I might as well have said I'm a Pony Express rider.

Officially, "bush pilot" *is* passé; the Federal Aviation Administration now uses the term "air taxi" to refer to U.S. commercial pilots who fly small charter aircraft. But in remote areas of Alaska the older designation unofficially persists because the job pilots do there has changed little since aviation began in the north country almost three-quarters of a century ago. The bush pilot still provides groceries, mail, medical evacuations, and transportation for people who otherwise would have to travel by foot, boat, or snowmobile. He still lands at some places that don't even have names, let alone aeronautical facilities. He still flies by the seat of his pants in rain, wind, fog, and snow.

Alaskan literature includes many books and articles about bush flying in the great bulk of the state between the Gulf of Alaska and the Arctic. This area contains Alaska's two largest population centers and was home to Bob Reeve, Noel Wien, and most other legendary pioneer aviators.

Less examined is bush aviation in the isolated southeastern region, or Southeast, as it's called. Yet Southeast bush flying is notable in several respects. For instance, nowhere in Alaska has progress less touched bush flying than here. Ubiquitous mountains in Southeast limit the use of the modern electronic navigational aids that help more northern pilots find their way to bush destinations in the much flatter Interior and Arctic. Southeast's rugged terrain also inhibits construction of airports, and its thick forests and spongy muskeg leave few natural landing sites for wheel-plane pilots. Since virtually all Southeast habitation is by salt water any-way, the floatplane continues to dominate here more than anywhere else in the state. Some pilots who learned to fly in Southeast have never handled an airplane on wheels.

Pilots who have worked throughout Alaska generally agree that flying on floats in the mountainous geography and wet, windy weather of South-east constitutes the toughest bush flying in the state. They also agree that Southeast compensates with the greatest scenery and romantic color. Some pilots find the job overwhelming and quit after several weeks or months. Most manage to keep the challenges and rewards in reasonable balance for several years. Few pilot linger in this business past the age of forty.

While the following pages are a personal account of modern South-east bush flying, my experiences over seven years and 6000 hours in the cockpit are typical. All the incidents and people mentioned are real. I regret that the limited space available in one volume necessitated the omission of countless anecdotes that have enriched Southeast aviation over the years. Like my peers who are still flying, I deeply lament the deaths of so many comrades; in most cases they were unluckier, not less skilled, than the rest of us. If we could, we'd also change the rain, the long hours, the insecurity, the close calls, and all the other ogres we grumble about. Bush flying then would be more enjoyable – and less memorable.

A few notes about terminology. "The bush" refers to any remote, sparsely developed area, be it forest, jungle, desert, or plains. "Seaplane" is any aircraft designed to operate from the water. "Floatplane" is a sea-plane with floats (pontoons). "Flying boat" is a seaplane that uses its hull for flotation. "Amphibian" is an airplane that can operate from both the water and the land; wheels in the floats or the hull retract for wa-ter phases.

NO WOLVES
IN THE NEWSROOM

Eight hundred feet below, gusts whip around the trailers and corrugated tin buildings of the Cape Pole logging camp and fan out across the harbor in black microbursts, foam spraying off the whitecaps. Twenty-five, maybe thirty knots. I grimace in disgust. Two hours earlier the Cape Pole camp manager had radioed our dispatcher in town that the wind was only ten to fifteen knots. "It's not too bad," he reported. "You guys have come out here in worse stuff than this."

Bush residents try to give accurate weather reports. But an observer peering out the window of a warm, dry, camp operations office usually perceives conditions to be more favorable than does a pilot circling overhead within the elements. In addition, when they want transportation bush residents tend to minimize the weather, aware that once a pilot has flown all the way out from town he'll often grudgingly land in conditions that would have kept him from taking off had he known about them.

Now I face that flying dilemma known as the marginal situation: conditions foul enough to pose serious concerns, yet not quite foul enough to make proceeding downright foolhardy.

Once, twice, three times I circle in the turbulence, squinting through the rain-streaked windshield, assessing, calculating. A green van moves slowly down the causeway below and stops at the top of the ramp by

1

the seaplane dock. Inside, I know, seven passengers and a driver are watching the de Havilland Beaver intently, urging me to land.

Marginal situations have confronted me repeatedly recently. Mid-November is usually a stormy period in southeastern Alaska, and this season mother nature obviously has no intention of breaking tradition. Day after day since—since forever, it seems—gales have howled in from the adjacent North Pacific, lashing the islands, the forest, the mountains, the communities. Some days none of the company's aircraft have turned a propeller. On others, our usual destinations have been marginally workable.

Cape Pole, by Sumner Strait on the west side of Kosciusko Island ninety miles northwest of my base in Ketchikan, has received no air service for almost a week now. Like most communities in Southeast, as Alaskans call this remote part of the state, the camp is accessible only by air or sea. Thus, the cabin behind me is stuffed with overdue mail sacks, cartons of groceries, choker cables, chain-saw blades, cases of beer, boxes of disposable diapers, replacement parts for machinery, and other cargo. In the van below my passengers wait impatiently for a ride to town. Their thoughts focus on shopping in stores or consulting a dentist or just escaping from the boondocks for a few days—not on the hazards of landing a floatplane in a gusty crosswind amid jagged reefs or taking off again with a heavy load.

Of course, I can avoid the hazards by retreating to town and reporting conditions were clearly unsafe. But avoiding my conscience would be impossible; conditions are not clearly unsafe. I am a bush pilot. My responsibility is to transport people and cargo in the wilderness. Stormy weather is part of the job.

Gritting my teeth, I throttle back, lower the flaps, and line up for a crosswind approach along the rock-free corridor by the shoreline.

"Ketchikan, Seven-Five Romeo, landing Cape Pole," I announce monotonically into the microphone.

A moment later the dispatcher's distant voice crackles in my headphones: "Roger, Seven-Five Romeo, landing Cape Pole."

Gusts jolt the Beaver like a giant's flicking finger as we descend, and I whip the control wheel left and right continuously to level the wings. I must also alternately jam the throttle forward and yank it back to counter the downdrafts and updrafts that shove the airplane around.

Five hundred feet, three hundred, one hundred. I am still uncommitted; I can still apply climb power and bank away. Remember, my mind warns, you not only have to get down, you have to take off crosswind

2

with some 1300 pounds of additional weight. I hold the Beaver off as long as possible to avoid the rougher water out from the camp and to squeeze a few more seconds for consideration. Then pilings, rocks, and trees loom too close in the windshield, and the option vanishes.

The floats thump onto the waves. The Beaver bounces heavily twice before shuddering off the step, the prop snarling from saltwater spray. As I taxi in, the airplane sways drunkenly in the choppy water.

At the dock I cut the engine, and two rainsuit-clad men from the van grab the wing line and strut while I scramble out to tie the float's mooring line to a cleat on the dock.

"Howdy," I mutter. "Beautiful weather."

"Glad to see you!" one of the men answers. Six other people emerge from the van at the top of the ramp, hunching against the driving rain. They pull suitcases, handbags, and a couple of sacks of mail from the vehicle and lug them down the ramp.

With one of the loggers on the float and another on the dock forming a relay line, I hand out item after item until at last the cabin is empty. The men then pass up the baggage and mail sacks, which I cram into the luggage compartment and under and behind the rear, hammock-style row of seats.

"I'll turn you out," the van driver says moments later, when the four men, two women, and child are strapped into their seats. He clutches the tip of the tail's left horizontal stabilizer while I slam the cabin door, untie the line, and climb in through the cockpit door. The nose of the Beaver immediately weathervanes from the dock in the crosswind, the tail serving as a pivot. I start the engine anad the driver releases the tail. As we taxi out, moisture from wet clothing fogs the windshield and all six side windows. I hold my door open for circulation and pass back the roll of paper towels, asking the passengers not to use their hands to wipe away the fog.

"Didn't think we was ever gonna get to town again," comments the man in the right front seat as he rotates a towel across his window. He grins, showing tobacco-stained teeth. Rain droplets glisten on his beard.

Flaps, takeoff position. Prop control, high RPM. Mixture control, full rich. Fuel selector, front tank. Elevator trim, set for an aft center of gravity.

"Everybody have a seatbelt?" I ask. A rush of nods and smiles follows. "Okay, let's go to Ketchikan."

My heart thumping, I pull up the water-rudders retraction handle and push the throttle to the redline at thirty-seven inches of manifold pressure. The idling of the 450-horsepower Pratt & Whitney engine deepens to a roar. As the Beaver lunges into the waves and struggles onto the step with a constant shuddering, a sense of doom engulfs me. The old airplane cannot possibly survive such a pounding with this load. Surely this time I have pushed too much. Transfixed by the waves and adjacent reefs, my mind sees flailing arms in the water by a broken, capsized airplane.

While the waves jolt my buttocks, the wind hammers the airplane from the side, jostling the tail and right wing. I fight back with aileron and rudder, an acrobat swinging a balancing pole on a wiggling tightrope. On and on we thump across the waves.

Then, the vibrating through the airframe begins to diminish, and I sense a lighter feel on the controls. The wings are gathering lift as the Beaver slowly picks up speed. I find myself coaxing the airplane in a whisper: "Come on, baby, come on, come on, fly!"

The floats are skimming the crests now. At last we stagger into the air. Instantly the crosswind jerks the Beaver sideways, and I must crab some thirty degrees into it to maintain a straight course. Turbulence shakes and rolls the Beaver, but the floatplane plows doggedly upward. When we reach 500 feet I turn inland over the clearcut stumps, scratch, and logging roads of Kusciusko Island, dodging frequent patches of scud. I notice that the logger next to me grips the bottom of his seat. He is no longer grinning. I don't have to turn around to know the other passengers are also holding on.

"Ketchikan, Seven-Five Romeo, Cape Pole inbound."

"Roger, Seven-Five Romeo, Cape Pole for Ketchikan. How is it out there?"

"Windy and rainy."

As it was yesterday, and the day before, as it will undoubtedly be tomorrow and the following day. Suddenly, I realize how weary I am of the gusty wind and the relentless rain and the dirty gray scud racing by just overhead. Weary of marginal situations and the pressure they bring. Weary of the long, long summer days, when I take off for yet another flight while normal people are sitting down to dinner. Weary of floatplanes and wilderness and bush people.

Gone is the sense of romance that compelled me to leave newspaper reporting for bush flying. Like a disillusioned infantryman, I now feel only battle fatigue. Perhaps the time has come to get out. With a degree in journalism and three years' experience on a daily paper, I should be able to find another job. The country has hundreds of newspapers and magazines. I am still young. I can tell prospective editors the adventure is out of my blood and that now I'm ready—no, eager—to resume my career.

My timing for such escape is perfect. Business has slowed considerably in the past few weeks with the stormy autumn weather and the end of seasonal industries like tourism and commercial fishing. I can give notice as soon as we land in Ketchikan and be excused from duty by next week—maybe even the end of this week. Tonight I'll draft a résumé and prepare a portfolio of my clippings.

The decision made, I spend the next few minutes thinking about working behind a desk in a white-collar shirt and tie in a warm, dry, secure newsroom. The daydream makes my present world seem even more hostile when I return to it. The Beaver is over Sea Otter Sound now, plodding along at a groundspeed of just seventy knots against the stiff headwind. Below, foaming waves churn the water into a maelstrom that would tear the airplane apart in a forced landing. A mile to the southwest, swells surge rhythmically onto the rocks of little Whale Head Island and explode in huge white sheets that shoot into the air as if trying to slap the base of the overcast.

I can now discern the foggy outline of Heceta Island ahead. As we gradually approach its hills and mountains, the buffeting intensifies. I crossed Heceta through Warm Chuck Inlet on the way out, but a shower now casts an impenetrable curtain of gloom across that shortcut; I will have to follow the shoreline around. When we reach the edge of the shower, thickening rain begins pummeling the windshield, and the cabin darkens as if we've flown into dusk. I descend to 300 feet, then 200, and turn east to parallel the shoreline. Rocky islets, nameless coves, and stands of trees slide by like ghosts a few yards off the right wingtip. I throttle back to low cruise power and extend the flaps to slow down.

"Wipe off your side window," I tell the bearded logger next to me, rubbing my paper towel across the inside of the windshield. But the air vents have long since dispelled the fog on the windows; the misty gray murk outside cannot be lightened with a paper towel.

Near the eastern tip of Heceta, islets begin appearing off the left wingtip. I lean forward against my seatbelt, squinting. I have followed this shoreline in similar conditions before, but familiarity doesn't make threading an airplane through a foggy maze of islets at low altitude any more comfortable. A wrong turn, a momentary loss of visibility in a concentrated downpour . . .

Now the mass of Tuxekan Island materializes ahead. I turn down the channel separating the two islands, then southwest into Tonewek Narrows toward Prince of Wales Island. Near a fading pictograph ancient Tlingit Indians painted on a rock wall, a vicious downdraft pops the microphone off its hook on the instrument panel. My right-seat passenger's arms flail in alarm.

Visibility here drops to a quarter mile. I cannot yet pick out Prince of Wales, although I know the 130-mile-long island lies just off the left wing. I descend to fifty feet so I can chop the throttle and land if necessary. But in a few seconds the island dutifully forms in the windshield, and I begin following the Prince of Wales shoreline. Driftwood jumbled at the high-tide line, part of an old skiff, a marten scampering back into the forest, dark little niches, seagulls pecking at a dead salmon, and other vignettes catch the edge of my vision as the Beaver lumbers along the rocky beach.

Not until we reach San Alberto Bay does the visibility return to two or three miles. I increase the power, retract the flaps, and climb back to the base of the clouds. Eight hundred feet is a low cruising altitude for an airplane, even a bush plane; aircraft in the landing pattern at an airport typically maintain 1000 feet. But after twenty minutes of wave-skimming, 800 feet seems luxuriously high, a dollar bill to an indigent panhandling for coins.

Suddenly I smell the nauseating odor of vomit and glance behind. Sitting in the middle seat of the rear row, the child, a girl of about ten, is doubled over, her head between her knees. A woman beside her holds her shoulders.

"There's a sick sack in the back of each seat," I yell, unable to see whether she already has one. "Whoever has the roll of paper towels, please pass it to her." If I am lucky, the girl has anticipated airsickness and prepared for it with an open bag. If not . . . Bush flying affords no flight attendants, no catering or clean-up crews. The pilot loads freight, pumps leakage water from the floats, fuels, empties the ashtrays, polishes the windows, and, whenever necessary, mops up after airsick passengers.

In a newsroom, I won't even have to empty my own wastebasket.

"Another forty-five minutes and we'll be in town," I shout over my shoulder to reassure the passengers. Silently, I add the proviso, "if we get through the pass." The Harris River valley—*the* pass to Ketchikan pilots—is the normal route across Prince of Wales, which separates Ketchikan and the majority of bush communities in this part of Southeast. It was marginally open on the flight to Cape Pole. I cannot see far enough ahead through the rain and scud to tell whether conditions there have improved or deteriorated, but we'll soon find out.

We rumble past the Tlingit village of Klawock, a mishmash of old dilapidated buildings, new government clapboard ones, a cannery, and fishing boats. Two minutes later we cross the outlet of Klawock Lake. I curse when I see that a wall of rainfog obscures the upper half of the six-mile-long lake, where the Harris River pass begins. We are down to 600 feet when we reach the head. Too low. I circle, peering into the pass, hoping to spot a hole. Nothing. Wait! Part of a hill seems visible where the pass makes a dogleg, about half a mile in. If so, that's enough visibility to go in and take a look. There will be room by the hill to turn around and fly back out if the valley beyond the dogleg is clobbered with clouds.

I circle again for another look but fail to resight the hill. A third circle. There! The hill, if it is indeed a hill, appears only from an angle by the north side of the lake, a darkish apparition within the misty curtain. An illusion? An area of heavier rain? If I take the bait and find only dense fog, we'll be trapped; at 600 feet the slopes along the upper end of the pass leave too little room in which to turn, and of course there is no place to land in the trees below. I circle one more time. Another marginal situation. No, less than marginal. This is the best pass, but not the only one.

I fly back down the lake and turn south. We bounce past the fishing community of Craig, which occupies a small island connected by a man-made peninsula to Prince of Wales, then follow the shoreline through a downpour in a fifteen-mile curve into Trocadero Bay. Above the head of the bay, a saddle in a heavily logged ridge leads to Twelve-Mile Arm on the east side of Prince of Wales, from which Ketchikan is a relatively easy over-water flight. The saddle lies a few hundred feet higher than the Harris River pass, but sometimes it offers better weather.

Not today. Solid clouds hold us relentlessly to 300 feet. We cannot leave the water, much less climb up the slope to peek over the saddle. There are several other passes to the south, near the Haida Indian village of Hydaburg, but clouds also blockade the valley we would have to cross to reach them. To follow a water route to the Hydaburg area would mean a long, circuitous flight through several clusters of islets and narrow channels close to the open sea, where the wind would be even stronger. If we negotiate that gauntlet and find the southern passes also closed, not enough fuel will remain to return for another look at the Harris River pass. Aviation gas weighs six pounds a gallon; at Ketchikan I pumped just thirty minutes' reserve fuel into the tanks knowing I'd have a heavy takeoff from Cape Pole.

I throttle back to twenty-eight inches of manifold pressure and 1750 RPM to reduce fuel consumption, then bank 180 degrees and work my way back toward Klawock Lake, calculating. At that power setting the engine burns about twenty-two gallons an hour. The rear and center tanks are empty, while the front one contains no more than twenty gallons. We are about to dig into our safety margin.

"Ketchikan, Seven-Five Romeo."

"Seven-Five Romeo, Ketchikan, go ahead."

"Peggy, we're by Klawock and having some trouble getting through. Has anybody else made it lately, or is anyone on the other side trying?"

"Negative. We're holding due to weather on your side. Keep us advised."

High-frequency radio waves can bend around obstructions and sometimes reach a receiver hundreds of miles away. Thus, the mountains are unable to isolate us from Peggy Acorn's somber voice. I picture the twenty-five-year-old brunette in her tiny dispatching cubicle, sipping a cup of coffee and chatting with one or more pilots but ever aware of who is en route to what destination and when he should be back. We are "her" pilots. She dispatches us into the elements to wilderness places she knows only by name or photo. For that authority she assumes the responsibility for making sure we return safely, or at least are accounted for satisfactorily. Although she can do nothing to help me cross Prince of Wales except relay pertinent reports from other pilots, I know she flies with us vicariously and will not go home until we land safely. We are not totally alone out here.

As we reapproach the Harris River pass, a hand taps me on the shoulder.

"I can't take this anymore," says the woman in the right seat of the middle row. Homely and overweight, she stares at me with wide-eyed desperation. She holds on to the top of the seat in front of her.

Well, ma'am, I too am feeling tension from the long battle with the weather, and I sympathize with you. But if I could divert to someplace where the wind would kick us less persistently and the rain and fog were less intense, we'd be there now. Unfortunately, southern California is a little beyond our fuel capacity. I could help you relax by not circling so close to the trees, but then we'd have less of a chance of finding a hole in the clouds and we'd have to spend the night out here in the boondocks instead of in town, where there are lots of people and lights and stores. Besides, you've flown in floatplanes before in this country. You ought to know by now that the risk is just something you have to tolerate, like the weather itself. If it's any consolation, I've also known fear— more than once. I've been so scared I've pleaded, "Oh dear god! Oh dear god!" repeatedly under my breath, and afterward wouldn't pick up the microphone because my passengers might have noticed the trembling of my hand. Rest assured that I don't want to be crushed and torn by the Beaver's 5000 pounds of metal any more than you do. Like you, I've got a lot to look forward to; I'm going to resume my career in journalism, and I want to do so in one piece. Also rest assured that I've been here before. I know how close to fly to the clouds and trees to make progress or to see if progress is possible and yet avoid that sudden, violent, fiery cessation of flight pilots and passengers alike experience many times in the mind. Let's try not to consider the fact that several fellow pilots far more seasoned than I experienced such violence in reality.

I force a smile to mask my own tension and turn my head sideways. "Don't worry. This isn't much fun, but I'm not going to fly into any granite clouds, and the turbulence can't hurt a Beaver. When we take you back to camp we'll arrange for some sunshine and blue sky."

The woman smiles weakly and settles acquiescently back in her seat.

The front fuel gauge now indicates only enough fuel to reach town, plus about fifteen minutes. That means one more try at the Harris River. If the pass is still impenetrable, we will have to land at Klawock and wait for better conditions—which, according to the Ketchikan Flight Service Station forecast this morning, are two days away. Instead of fire and dungeons, maybe hell is spending eternity trying to cross a stormy Prince of Wales Island in a floatplane.

The darkish apparition deep in the mist of the dogleg still beckons, and the ceiling seems a little higher, maybe 700 feet now. Heavy rain wouldn't have stayed in the same spot. I lower the flaps, snuggle as close to the north slope as possible, and enter. For a few moments adrenaline races through my veins as I struggle to see into the wall ahead, wondering whether I have brought us into a foggy cul-de-sac. Downdrafts swirling over the peaks hidden in the clouds above hammer the Beaver, and behind me I hear someone shriek.

Then, the unmistakable outline of a hill forms in front. I breathe deeply. I follow the dogleg around the hill and, staying to the side for room to turn, glance down the valley. Three-quarters of a mile, maybe a full mile. Okay so far. But the clouds begin sloping toward the surface after a couple of minutes, and when we reach the mouth of the river they intercept the treetops. I curse to myself, bank to turn, and immediately spot salt water through a small hole. We're home. Now we can follow the shoreline at wave-top level the final thirty-five miles to town, if necessary.

9

But it is not. As if the weather gods have conceded defeat, this side of Prince of Wales shows us a gentler world than we have endured the last hour and a half. Visibility here balloons to ten miles in a mere drizzle from a ceiling of at least 1500 feet. The wind produces only a light chop. In the distance the hills along Kasaan Peninsula look soft and green, scattered puffs of fog clinging like wispy fingers to their slopes. I point the nose on a direct course for town and climb to 1000 feet.

"Ketchikan, Seven-Five Romeo, we're through."

"Roger, Seven-Five Romeo, see you shortly."

Then, over my shoulder, I announce: "Another twenty minutes and we'll be on the water."

That good news, along with the conspicuously improved weather, transforms the atmosphere among the passengers. The bearded man in the right front seat lights a cigarette; chatter emanates from the cabin behind. Relieved myself, savoring the thought that soon I will never again have to fly floatplanes in the rain, fog, and wind, I too feel an impulse to talk.

"How much longer is Cape Pole going to operate this fall?" I ask the logger.

"Oh, that kinda depends on the weather," he answers through a mouthful of smoke. "We'll keep going as long as we can, till it snows. Then we'll pack up till spring. Man, that was some ride, huh!"

"Piece of cake."

The exchange fails to develop into a conversation, and he returns to his thoughts. My mind puts me back at a typewriter in a newsroom. Which publications shall I approach first? Free now from the exigencies of weather-flying, I ponder that question while absently sightseeing.

No bush pilot tires of studying the country, because even along familiar routes it always shows change, subtle or overt. The lazy stream of yesterday is a rushing, spilling freshet from the rain today. A formerly unremarkable hillside is now scarred with a brand new landslide, uprooted hemlock trees piled at the bottom of the swath. Fall colors seem a little brighter in the bushes along Old Frank's Lake.

And a muskeg meadow near the mouth of Coal Bay now contains several foreign objects.

Blacktail deer. I spot deer on most flights and ordinarily pay little attention to them. Wildlife always thrills passengers, however. These seven have had a rough flight; taking a few extra minutes to give them a close-up look at the deer will be good public relations.

"There are some deer down there right in the open," I yell over my shoulder. "Anybody want to take a look at them?"

The passengers nod their approval, and one man begins rummaging in a travel bag, presumably for a camera. I throttle back and descend, circling wide to come in low for a close view.

"They'll be on the left side," I call back. "One look's all we'll have before they dart into the forest."

The deer are on the nose now, about a quarter-mile ahead. I count four, clustered in the center of the muskeg by some jack pine. I squint to see whether any have antlers. Then, with a start I realize I am looking not at deer but at wolves.

"Wolves!" the logger next to me exclaims at the same moment, lightly jabbing me on the shoulder.

"Hey, they're wolves!" I tell the rest of the passengers. Those on the far right side of the cabin unfasten their seatbelts and crowd with the others by the windows on the left. The wolves, three with dirty brown-and-white coats and the fourth with a grayish black one, stand by what appears to be the carcass of a deer. As we rumble by they look up, tongues hanging out, resembling four big friendly huskies. I circle around again. This time as we approach the muskeg their rumps are disappearing into the sanctuary of the forest. I fly by the spot and bank steeply, hoping to look straight down on them, but the thickly bunched trees have swallowed them.

No matter. The animals have posed for one clear, stirring view. While wolf sightings are routine in the open country of the Alaskan interior, they prompt gasps in the dense forest of Southeast. So far in my bush-flying career, I have spotted hundreds of deer, mountain goats, and black bears, and dozens of grizzlies, but my previous wolf sightings number just two, each a shadowy glimpse in patchy woods. The cagey, elusive wolf—archvillain of folklore, enigmatic symbol of wilderness, perennial subject of controversy between conservationists and sportsmen. And, for me, a source of renewed appreciation for a unique lifestyle.

As I climb and resume a beeline for Ketchikan, I realize I am smiling, enriched by a zoological windfall. When I try to think again about a career change, I recall instead some of the other special moments bush flying has brought: exploring a long-abandoned Indian fish camp with my passengers, listening to a seventy-seven-year-old retired woodsman tell stories in his cabin, watching killer whales attack a colony of sea lions . . .

In Ketchikan I arranged for a month's vacation, and a week later flew commercially to my home on the East Coast. There I spent hours strolling along the deserted, windswept beaches of Long Island Sound, pondering my future, wondering if I was really ready for a more conventional lifestyle. Refreshed, I returned to Southeast, determined to continue flying.

Like the moods of weather, such disenchantment and renewed fascination with bush flying come in fairly regular cycles. You curse the hardships continually for a few days or weeks or months, then go through another period in which you wouldn't trade jobs with anyone on earth.

Ultimately—inevitably, perhaps—a period of disenchantment coincided with a lucrative job offer in journalism, and I resigned. Three and a half months later I was back in the cockpit of a floatplane. The next time I managed to stay away four years, and the time after that a year and a half. Despite the promises of a new life in a distant, bustling city, each escape attempt eventually emptied my spirit. My work would become meaningless drudgery, my surroundings colorless monotony.

Then, like a mythological siren singing seductively, the irresistible lure of bush flying would begin filling the void. I would spend more and more time reminiscing about Southeast and Ketchikan, about how a Connecticut greenhorn like me became a bush pilot, about the adventure I had forsaken. And about the fact that there are no wolves to sight in a newsroom.

THE SIREN CALLS

The newcomer to Ketchikan usually doesn't notice floatplanes right away. First—if he's lucky enough to arrive on a nice day—he admires the scenery; snowcapped, 3000-foot Deer Mountain behind town dwarfs everything else and automatically draws the eye. Next, the newcomer observes that this community of 11,000 is long and narrow, like a reclining basketball player. Houses that extend inland seem to cling precariously to steep forested slopes, often with long wooden staircases rather than streets for access. The cluttered waterfront that stretches along the length of the town then attracts the newcomer's attention. It is now that he notices the floatplanes, mixed among piers, docks, pilings, breakwaters, and every type of boat from skiff to ocean-going trawler.

I had never seen a floatplane before arriving in Ketchikan in late 1971 to work as a reporter for the Ketchikan *Daily News*. As the state ferry *Taku* sliced through the waters of Tongass Narrows toward Ketchikan's ferry landing, I counted more than a dozen floatplanes tied up by docks along the waterfront. Several others sat out of the water on wooden ramps. One orange-and-white floatplane was taxiing out for takeoff. Grimacing against the brisk November wind on my face, I watched as it roared down the Narrows like a speedboat and lifted ponderously into the air, spray trailing from each float. Seagulls in its path flapped wildly to get out of the way.

The reason for so many floatplanes in this part of the world had already become clear. Early that morning I had pulled into the port city of Prince Rupert, British Columbia, ninety miles to the south, after an eight-day drive from my home in Connecticut. All that remained of my journey then was a six-hour voyage up the Inside Passage to southeastern Alaska, the 500-mile-long chain of islands and narrow strip of mainland that extend like a panhandle from the main bulk of the state.

Exhausted but excited, I had spent much of this final leg out on deck sightseeing. On the mainland and many of the surrounding islands, huge mountains rose sharply from the sea to fade into a high overcast. A lush green forest covered every piece of terrain except for scattered muskeg patches and rocky slopes. In places the trees or cliffs descended right down to the waterline. Where beaches did show, they were strewn with rocks and driftwood.

The pilot of a wheel-equipped airplane would have had trouble finding even an emergency landing site in such a rugged environment. On floats, however, a pilot could casually touch down on coves, bays, inlets, fjords, or any of the other countless natural "runways" I had noticed. Maybe the major communities here had airports, but otherwise this majestic archipelago was indeed floatplane country.

Nonetheless, I was unimpressed. A licensed private pilot since my freshman year in college, I had earned my wings as a landlubber. Now I scoffed as the orange-and-white Beaver disappeared around an island with those ugly, cumbersome pontoons hanging down like silver torpedoes. Real airplanes had wheels.

As the resident pilot on the newspaper's four-person editorial staff, however, I inherited the aviation beat. In a few weeks I knew most of the town's twenty-five-odd air taxi floatplane pilots. There was the legendary Ed Todd of Todd's Air Service, who flew in short pants and bare feet in weather that grounded other pilots. Dixie Jewett, Todd's assistant, was the only female commercial pilot in town; according to Todd, she was better than most of the men. I also met Ketchikan Air's Don Ross, who had become a World War II fighter pilot before he was old enough to vote. An avid prospector, Ross was credited with making the first floatplane landing on a glacier in the Ketchikan area. Quiet, bespectacled Pete Cessnun, owner of Webber Air, held the distinction of being the second American called for duty after the draft was instituted in 1940; a vegetable clerk in a Kansas City cafeteria at the time, he and fellow employees were gathered around the radio when President Roosevelt read his number. Bud Bodding of the old Ellis Air Lines had the nickname "Father Goose" because he had logged more time in the twin-engine Grumman Goose amphibian than any other pilot in the world; he had stopped counting at 12,000 hours fifteen years earlier. Thanks to his savvy and especially sharp vision, Webber Air chief pilot Herman Ludwigsen had a knack for finding overdue airplanes. One discovery had earned him a $10,000 reward from the victim's family.

A hearty joie de vivre radiated from these and other pilots, and before long I began making the rounds at the air services along the waterfront more often than necessary—and lingering long after I had collected my intended notes and photos.

One day Earl Lahmeyer, a tall, studious partner in Ketchikan Air Service, invited me to ride along on a flight to the Tsimpshian Indian village of Metlakatla, seventeen miles away on Annette Island. The gentle swaying as the Cessna 185 taxied out and the vibrant tapping of the floats on the waves during takeoff erased whatever prejudice against floatplanes I still harbored. Two days later, stocky, arrogant Carl "Red" Jackson, owner of Revilla Flying Service, also offered me an unoccupied seat on a flight to Metlakatla.

Both men were to die in floatplane crashes.

My rounds produced enough regular grist to start a weekly aviation column. But merely writing about flying and making an occasional flight as an observer now left me hungry.

My own chance to fly floatplanes resulted from a unique newspaper beat. Twice a month publisher Lew M. Williams, Jr., sent two or three staff members to the fishing towns of Wrangell and Petersburg, 80 and 110 miles northwest of Ketchikan, to gather stories and ads for a monthly regional magazine the newspaper published. Because of inconvenient airline and ferry schedules, these trips sometimes took three days, and often the staffers had to leave some work undone to catch the ride home. Charter flights offered flexibility but were too expensive. A rented floatplane, on the other hand, would save both time and money if the paper could supply the pilot.

Since I was already a licensed wheelplane pilot, Williams decided to invest in a seaplane rating for me. Jack Cousins, who had flown for the old Simpson Air in Ketchikan before switching to millwright work at the local pulp mill, offered Ketchikan's only flight instruction and rental floatplane. A stocky, jovial man, Cousins kept his yellow-and-white

Cessna 172 at Brusich Marina north of town.

In the air a floatplane handles just like a wheelplane, except that it's a bit slower due to the aerodynamic drag of the floats. On the water, however, a floatplane is subject to the same forces as a boat. Although I had grown up just a few miles from Long Island Sound, I had spent most of my recreational hours on tennis courts, and Cousins discovered a few minutes into my first lesson that I knew nothing about boating.

The 172 sat berthed at an angle on a wooden ramp with its tail toward the water. As we conducted a preflight inspection of the airplane, Cousins pointed to the green, slime-like algae that coated the lower part of the ramp, where it met the water.

"Step on that stuff and you'll fall on your ass so fast you won't know what happened," he warned.

For a few moments I remembered. In preparation for getting the airplane off the ramp, we removed the tiedown lines, and Cousins attached a long line to the right rear float strut. Then we pushed and rocked on the bows of the floats. Inch by inch the 172 slid down the ramp on its float keels. Our boots drew closer and closer to the algae. Suddenly, my feet shot out from under me and I plopped onto the ramp with a splash, my buttocks and legs in the cold water. Cursing, I scrambled to my feet and brushed at my trousers.

"Well, now you've been initiated," Cousins said, chuckling.

With a final push we backed the 172 into the water. When momentum had carried it about ten feet from the ramp, Cousins yanked the long line, spinning the airplane around so that the tail now pointed toward us. He then hauled the 172 back in, lifted on the lower rear fuselage, and walked up the ramp a couple of feet until the heels of the floats slid onto the planking.

"There," he said.

The process looked uncomplicated, but on my own I found it an art requiring both finesse and planning. If you yank the long line too lightly, the airplane stops pivoting when it's perpendicular to the ramp. Then you must haul it in sideways and turn it the rest of the way by hand. If the airplane leaves the ramp with insufficient momentum, yanking on the line fails to have a full pivoting effect and instead pulls the machine off to the side, perilously close to a piling or another ramped floatplane. Of course, the wind and current can frustrate the most careful planning.

And always the green algae lurks by the water; step too close while absorbed in maneuvering the airplane around and swoosh—down you go.

Once the floatplane is tailed back up on the ramp, the pilot removes the long turning line, then steps from the ramp onto the left float, walks along it to the cockpit door and climbs in. The passengers do the same on the right side. A floatplane has no brakes. The first time I taxied off the ramp in Cousins's 172 I nearly jammed the toes of the rudder pedals, which activate brakes on most wheelplanes, through the floor in an attempt to slow down when a Boston Whaler suddenly zipped across our path.

"In a floatplane," Cousins patiently explained, "you reduce taxiing speed by throttling back. You can do S-turns to get around an obstruction or to give yourself more time. If you're going into the wind, lowering the flaps or opening the doors will present more surface to the wind to blow against, helping you slow down. If you have to stop, shut off the engine and water friction will do the job. Remember, you're a sailor now."

We taxied around for a few minutes while I got the feel of maneuvering on the water. Then it was time to learn how to dock. I had watched the commercial pilots shut off the engine as they approached the dock. When the left float nudged the bumpers, the pilots casually stepped out and tied up the plane.

"I know how to do it," I told Cousins, hoping to redeem myself for my display of marine ignorance. But I cut the engine too late, and the 172 glided swiftly by the dock before I could clamber out and stop it. I restarted the engine and came around for another try. This time I cut the engine too soon, and we stopped dead in the water some ten feet from the dock. I looked at Cousins sheepishly.

"Well," he said, "get the paddle, get out on the float, and paddle us in."

Once I had gained a reasonable degree of basic competence on the water, I graduated to takeoffs and landings. I had thought both would be fairly simple because of the ample "runway" a floatplane pilot has, but my seaplane schooling was teaching me repeatedly that handling an airplane on the water involves more considerations than an observer realizes. While a wheelplane simply charges down the runway, a floatplane has to get "on the step" before it can become airborne—it has to attain enough water speed so that the weight of the airplane is supported by hydrodynamic pressure on the steps, or bottoms, of the floats rather than by the floats' buoyancy, much as a speedboat rides on the step above a certain speed.

First, the wheel is held back for a nose-high attitude so that water pressure will force the bows of the floats out of the water as takeoff power is applied. Then, as speed starts to build, the wheel is eased forward to help the airplane climb from this "plowing" stage onto the step. The airplane accelerates quickly once it is on the step, and the pilot holds the nose at a slightly high attitude until the floats leave the water. Pressure on the wheel changes throughout the takeoff process; more than any instrument reading or external visual cue, it is the feel of the wheel that the pilot uses as a guide.

In the air, Cousins showed me how to "read" the water for wind direction by looking at the curvature of the waves, at foam sliding off the upwind side of crests, and at the lee and windward shores of a point or peninsula. He taught me to circle before landing to scout for driftwood and rocks. I learned to land parallel to swells to avoid the skipping that results from landing across them. I learned to make a gradual, power-on, nose-up approach over glassy water because depth perception is virtually nil without some disturbance on the surface. I learned to make turns while taxiing on the step only from upwind to downwind, so that centrifugal force and the wind would cancel each other and minimize the chance of capsizing.

And I learned the art of sailing backwards to a dock or beach, a necessary maneuver when a floatplane is upwind of the destination and the wind is too strong to turn out of it. Like a juggler, the pilot manipulates throttle, rudder, ailerons, and flaps to control drift speed and angle. Depending on skill, sailing into a tight spot between boats, pilings, or other floatplanes can be a satisfying accomplishment or an expensive mistake.

Reramping the 172 at the end of our session involved lining up with the ramp while compensating for the drift of the current and wind, and running the airplane onto the planks with power. At first, leery of propelling the airplane over the top of the ramp and into the pilings beyond, I used the throttle too gingerly; the 172 would stop half in and half out of the water. We then had to shut off the engine, push the airplane back into the water, and try again. Eventually I discovered the proper touch.

After ten hours of instruction—all in good weather—I took and passed a checkride for a seaplane rating with Jim Rockman, a lanky, bespectacled Ketchikan Police Department lieutenant who moonlighted as a designated flight examiner for the Federal Aviation Administration.

"Here's your ticket," Rockman said afterward, handing me the approval form. "But remember: your education in float flying has just begun."

Rockman's caution was superfluous; while the new rating brought pride, it also gave me the butterflies a newly licensed driver feels when thinking about the local expressway. I had spent enough time listening to commercial pilots talk about their misadventures to realize I was a Southeast aviation cheechako (an Alaskan term for newcomer).

The newspaper now began renting Cousins's 172 for me to fly to Wrangell and Petersburg twice a month with a couple of advertising sales people. Sometimes I'd scrub a flight two or three days in a row before mother nature provided the fair skies I wanted. Although one of my training sessions had included a familiarization flight to the two communities, I flew with a chart unfolded on my lap and navigated by the easiest routes, whether or not they were the shortest ones. At each stop I refueled, even though the tanks had enough capacity for a round trip with a healthy reserve.

Wrangell was a sleepy town with a population of 2500. Originally the site of a Tlingit Indian village, the community sat on the tip of Wrangell Island near the mouth of the Stikine River. While the ad people delivered their spiel to merchants, I visited the city manager for a rundown on official happenings, then wandered about with my notebook and camera. I deemed the most interesting place in town to be at our starting point. Stikine Air Service, Wrangell's only air taxi, was based in a hangar in the city harbor. It was there I tied up the 172.

Petersburg, off Frederick Sound on the north end of Mitkoff Island, had two air taxies, a Scandinavian heritage, and similar populations of people and seagulls.

From the Alaska Island Air dock, as from most points in town, the towering Coast Mountains on the mainland across Frederick Sound created a spectacular backdrop. When clouds and showers began obscuring the peaks, I rounded up the ad salespeople and took off for home, a skittish settler heading for the fort after seeing smoke signals on the horizon. In a country plagued by fickle weather, an encounter with the bad guys was inevitable.

Raindrops were already splattering on the windshield late one afternoon as we climbed out by the Petersburg waterfront. By the time we reached Behm Canal near Ketchikan, newly formed rain squalls surrounded us like antiaircraft flak. I zigzagged around one after another until we got to the eastern shore of the canal, where an apparent detour turned out to be a cul-de-sac that lured us into the heart of a massive squall. A driving deluge suddenly engulfed and buffeted the little 172, and I gripped the wheel like a lifeline. Visibility blurred myopically through the windshield. I throttled back and descended, my heart booming. Then the sky brightened, the buffeting subsided, and we emerged from the squall, shaken but relieved.

Later, as a full-time air taxi pilot, flying through rain squalls became routine. But perception of adventure is relative; even a flight in sunshine quickens the pulse of someone who has never been up in a small airplane.

Experience gradually increased my self-confidence and my appreciation of the challenge, the beauty, and the excitement of Alaskan floatplane flying. Sleep now tarried for hours the night before a flight, as it had years earlier the night before a visit to an amusement park. In the air, I dared to explore new, more direct routes to Wrangell and Petersburg. I descended to circle a pod of killer whales. I climbed to 10,000 feet to view the sweeping panorama of the snowcapped Coast Mountains. Near Petersburg I sneaked a quick excursion to picturesque Le Conte Glacier, which calved turquoise-colored icebergs into Le Conte Bay.

In the evening, the 172 back on the ramp securely tied down, I reveled in the richness of the day as my fellow workers and I strolled by the darkened boat sheds of Brusich Marina to our car.

During the days or weeks between flights I sat at my desk in the newsroom amid the clacking of manual typewriters and the clicking of the teletype machine, trying not to daydream. But the sirens of the bush whispered continuously. They had an ally in a large, dogeared map of Southeast thumbtacked on the wall directly across from my desk. I had only to raise my eyes to gaze at a world of romantic-sounding places off the Wrangell-Petersburg routes: Tombstone Bay, Hidden Inlet, Peril Strait, Escape Point, Cape Decision, Security Cove, Hole-in-the-Wall, Port Protection, Black Bear Lake . . . Especially when the sun shone through the large picture window up front by the reception counter, concentrating on an interesting story took determined self-discipline; a story on an economic-development seminar or last night's city council meeting had no chance at all.

As soon as my tenure at the newspaper qualified me for a vacation, I hurried down to Boeing Field in Seattle and took training for a commercial pilot's license. With the license carefully preserved in lamination in my wallet and 350 hours of total flight time (including nearly 50 hours of floatplane experience) religiously recorded in my logbook, I approached several air taxi operators in Ketchikan to ask for a job. Each smiled paternally.

"Fifty hours do not a floatplane pilot make, my son. We need seasoned, well-rounded pilots."

"Okay, I'll fly for free after work and on my days off until I have enough experience to join the payroll."

"Ah, but we have more at stake than pilots' salaries. Our reputation depends on professionalism and a good safety record. Those things come only with experience. Besides, our insurance company demands at least 500 hours total time. Why don't you buy yourself a puddle-jumper, fly the hell out of it for a year, then come back?"

A "puddle-jumper" is any old, small, low-powered, two-seat airplane whose main virtue is economy: Taylorcrafts, Cessna 140s, early Cessna 150s, and the like. Ed Todd of Todd's Air Service said he owned an ancient but airworthy Luscombe on floats he would sell me for just $4500. He had bought it several years earlier as a trainer for a high school student-friend who had since gotten a commercial job, and the airplane now sat uninsured on a ramp at the windy Peninsula Point seaplane moorage on the edge of town. With my savings, a bank loan, a loan from the paper, and a generous financing agreement from Todd, I managed to swing the deal.

The Luscombe was a 1939 8E model whose original fabric skin had been replaced with aluminum. The faded red-and-white paint peeled like eggshell in places, especially on the belly and tail, areas most susceptible to the sandblasting effects of saltwater spray. Inside, there were sticks instead of wheels, and exposed control cables ran through pullies on the cabin ceilings and sides. The spartan panel contained the minimum instruments required by FAA regulations. The two nonadjustable seats had little padding, and although I stood nearly six feet tall, I needed a cushion to see over the panel through the crazed, scratched windshield. Gaps around the doors let in drafts that rendered the cabin-heat control completely ineffective.

But no matter; the Luscombe was my escape into the world of adventure and romance I had come to cherish. No longer was I restricted to bimonthly flights to Wrangell and Petersburg in a rented 172. Now I had my own magic carpet, awaiting my commands whenever benign weather and free time coincided. For that luxury I gladly sacrificed the gilded edges.

After work and on weekends I taxied out of the harbor at the Peninsula Point seaplane moorage and took off to build flight time, usually with a companion. We explored villages, fjords, lighthouses, and other places. On many outings we landed in a lake and fished off the floats beneath steep, lush-green slopes. When our stomachs began growling we paddled the Luscombe to shore like a canoe and fried fresh trout for lunch.

While we always left Ketchikan with a favorable forecast, the weatherman offered no guarantees. One unscheduled overnighting in fog at a lake on Prince of Wales Island resulted in a visit the next morning by a huge Coast Guard rescue helicopter from the Annette Air Station.

If the end of a workday did not allow enough light for a flight, I often drove to Peninsula Point anyway to kick kelp off the ramp, sniff the sea breeze, and daydream.

During Southeast's frequent gales, I left the office under the frown of publisher Williams to hurry out and check the tiedown lines. Drenched from horizontal rain before I got ten feet from the parking lot, I often literally had to crawl across the boardwalk in the harbor to avoid being blown into the water by sixty- or seventy-knot gusts.

When my logbook finally reached the magic 500 hours, I again made the rounds of air services to ask for a flying job. This time I got one.

APPRENTICESHIP

The cargo bins lined the walls, twenty-four in all, twelve on each side in tiers of two. Above each was stenciled in black letters the name of a destination: Cape Pole, Port Alice, Craig, Hydaburg, Hyder . . . Some bins were stuffed to the rims with boxes, tires, crates, bundles of newspapers, mail sacks, fishing poles, logging cables, and other cargo, while a few contained just a handful of items. A counter faced the street door and abutted a desk littered with various forms and manifests.

This was the freight room, my new working home. Actually, it occupied a part of the hangar, with a clapboard wall separating it from the larger portion in which the mechanics worked. The other side of the freight room formed one wall of the building containing the operations office, ticket counter, passengers' waiting room, pilots' lounge, and accounting offices.

The company I had joined was the largest of seven air services in Ketchikan, with seven full-time and three part-time pilots, plus an assorted crew of reservationists, dispatchers, mechanics, lineboys, and bookkeepers. It operated four Cessna 185s, four de Havilland Beavers, a Grumman Goose, and a Cessna 180.

Unlike other pilots in town, ours wore airline-type uniforms, complete with hat, white shirt, black tie, gold epaulets, black shoes, and four

23

gold braids on the jacket sleeves. Other air taxi people throughout South-east wisecracked about the absurdity of uniformed bush pilots. After all, the profession involved such messy chores as fueling and oiling planes, handling greasy industrial freight, striding down muddy village streets to fetch a tardy passenger, and stepping into the water at the edge of a lake or cove to beach the aircraft.

But business was booming. The opening the year before of the new Ketchikan Airport on nearby Gravina Island had brought the company a windfall of daily scheduled flights to the fishing communities of Craig, Klawock, and Hydaburg on Prince of Wales Island. Alaska Airlines had used its fleet of twin-engine Grumman Goose amphibians for those runs and also to shuttle airliner passengers between the Ketchikan waterfront and the town's old, World War II airport on Annette Island, twenty-three miles away. The new airport, just a five-minute ferry ride across Tongass Narrows, had eliminated the need for the shuttle flights. The Prince of Wales flights alone could not support the Grumman fleet, so Alaska Airlines had decided to sell its Gooses and subcontract the Prince of Wales flights to us.

We had an aggressive advertising campaign, and our airplanes flew from dawn to well into the evening, day after day except when weather grounded us. The management foresaw continued growth and envisioned expansion into a regional airline. To achieve that goal, the company had to have the right image. Pilots dressed in the traditional checkered shirt, blue jeans, and rubber boots would no longer do.

Before signing on with the company, I too had joked about the uni-forms. But now, little higher than a lineboy, I regarded them as a status symbol; the right image included professionalism, and green, newly hired pilots like me had to serve an apprenticeship in the freight room so they could learn the day-to-day routine before earning the privilege of don-ning a uniform. Since my fellow "ramp rats" were unskilled teenagers and I was a twenty-nine-year-old journalist with a masters degree, a miffed ego shuffled with me behind the counter in the unheated freight room. Besides keeping track of freight and mail, my lot was to help the pilots dock, brush the aircraft wings and tails after a spring snow shower, help load and unload the planes, occasionally fuel a plane, and perform vari-ous maintenance chores.

But the apprenticeship wasn't entirely on the ground. Every two or three days chief pilot Dwight Gregerson sent me as an observer on a flight that had an empty seat. The forty-five-year-old Gregerson, slender, distinguished-looking, and congenial, admonished me against regarding the flights as breaks from the freight room monotony.

"Get to know the country," he said. "Look at how things are done. Ask the pilots questions. If you don't pay attention now, you'll wish you had when you're on your own out there."

Kirk Thomas, my first teacher at the company, had begun as a common lineboy several years earlier. Deciding he'd rather be a pilot, he took flying lessons and, with financial help from the company, earned a commercial pilot's license in the Lower Forty-eight. A hard-working Mormon farm boy from Utah with the build of a fullback, Thomas would own the company in a few years.

Some destinations, such as Craig, Klawock, and Hydaburg, and of course Wrangell and Petersburg, were familiar from my newspaper and Luscombe flights. But I had never flown to the more obscure hamlets and settlements, nor to the logging camps scattered over the vast upper half of Prince of Wales. And while my newspaper/Luscombe flights had waited for fair weather, air taxi flights enjoyed no such luxury. As Thomas followed the winding waterways and cut through narrow valleys by thawing ponds under low stratus in the Cessna 185, I tried to do the same with my finger on the chart in my lap.

"It all looks the same from down low," I told him. "I don't see how you can find your way without a map."

Thomas smiled. "I had to use a map for the first few weeks out here. Then it suddenly all just clicked together."

At forty-one, Chuck Collins was one of the oldest line pilots, and the most professional. He had previously flown Grumman Gooses for Alaska Airlines but had been furloughed when the new airport opened. An outgoing, talkative chainsmoker, Collins flew as if he had an FAA inspector on board every flight. He made long approaches and shallow banks and circled each destination before landing to look for obstructions, even at places he had already visited earlier in the day.

With passengers he smiled and catered and never lost patience. At first I assumed his display of caution and courtesy was exaggerated as a model for me, but I discovered that such was his style. In fact, the management periodically chided him for overdoing it, for taking too long to complete flights. But he continued his ways unfazed.

"They can call me a little old lady all they want," Collins told me one day over Prince of Wales. "I consider it a compliment."

Eventually, when his low seniority number finally reached the top of the recall list, Alaska rehired him as a flight engineer on 727 jets.

John "Big John" Bussanich, by contrast, horsed the 185 around like a fighter pilot. He buzzed a camp or a village before landing as if strafing it to let a passenger know the plane had arrived, and when he banked I wondered if we had entered a snap roll. Bussanich—tall and solid, with a thick mustache on a somber face that hinted of the Middle East—did not fly recklessly; he simply knew he was in a bush plane, not an airliner. Ketchikan-born, he had flown B-25 bombers in the South Pacific with the Army Air Corps; later he would fly business jets overseas.

There was handsome, arrogant Bob Ulrich, who, like the famous Wiley Post, had lost an eye but who managed to thread his way through a foggy pass more consistently than two-eyed pilots. Chief pilot Gregerson, one of the most experienced pilots in Southeast with 14,000 hours, had a maestro's touch that inspired instant confidence and admiration. Prone to occasional temper tantrums in which he yanked off his hat and threw it on the ground, Gregerson charmed his passengers like a master of ceremonies with a natural laugh and tactful banter. Gray-haired Keith Stigen, a retired air force master sergeant, retained the friendly, disciplined demeanor he had picked up in his first career. Young Andy Loud had transported field-grade officers in Beechcraft King Airs over the jungles of Vietnam as a U.S. Army pilot. Before moving to Ketchikan he had flown floatplanes for Lake Union Air Service in Seattle.

Each pilot had a different style, with me as well as with a bush plane. Collins took a few minutes at each stop to give me a quick walking tour of the camp or village, occasionally pausing to drop into an office for an introduction with the local manager or agent. Ulrich, who had an insatiable appetite, circled each camp to point out the location of the cookhouse and provided a commentary on its culinary virtues: "Norma bakes the best cookies in southeast Alaska; treat her like a queen when she flies to town."

A couple of pilots kept up a steady monologue of operational caveats: "Stay away from the west shoreline when you land because the water there is riddled with rocks." "There's no water to land in for six miles if you try to save time by flying through the notch in the mountain." "Don't fly anywhere near that goddamn cliff in a strong southeast wind, 'cause the downdrafts will shake your fillings out."

And a couple, preoccupied with their own thoughts, seemed oblivious to my presence and rarely uttered a word.

After two weeks, Gregerson began sending me out in the little Cessna 180 to make an occasional freight run when benign weather prevailed and the regular flights were unable to handle the accumulation in the bins. I also began making weekly contract-mail flights. One run went up west Behm Canal to a cabin in Deep Bay, the settlement of Loring, a logging camp in Neets Bay, and the fishing resorts at Bell Island and Yes Bay. A second run stopped at the Haida village of Kasaan in Kasaan Bay, an old cannery in Steamboat Bay on Noyes Island, and the fishing hamlet at Meyers Chuck, while the third went to the old mining town of Hyder at the head of Portland Canal by the British Columbian border.

Assistant Manager Art Hack, a retired naval aviator who had served a tour in the stormy Aleutian Islands, rode in the right-hand seat to introduce me to the mail runs. A stocky man with graying curly hair and narrow hooded eyes, Hack usually opened the facilities in the morning and locked them up at night, after the rest of us had gone home.

On the familiarization flight to Hyder, over the sweeping wilderness of the Coast Mountains still buried in winter white, I suddenly noticed he was sleeping. How long had his eyes been closed? I had thought his silence signaled affirmation of my navigation. The endless valleys and peaks around us looked alike to me, and I debated waking him. Then I decided that no one could miss a landmark as conspicuous as seventy-mile-long Portland Canal on a sunny day. For more visibility, I climbed until the altimeter read almost 9000 feet. Sure enough, a few minutes later Portland Canal appeared on the horizon. Now a gradual descent over the canal, keeping the power up to avoid a change in engine noise that might awaken Hack. I'd show him I could do the job unsupervised. Two settlements were evident at the head of the canal—Hyder and its neighbor, tiny Stewart, British Columbia. I glanced at my slumbering copilot again and again, hoping he would remain asleep until I landed. What better demonstration of my ability than this!

The seaplane dock was conspicuous at the end of a long causeway three miles ahead. Slowly, slowly, I eased back the throttle as I lost altitude, paying little attention to the magnificent scenery lining the canal. The wind was calm, the water flat. Plenty of time to grease the 180 on smoothly. A notch of flaps. Keep the nose up, don't fly into the glassy water. A second notch of flaps. A third. Power back a hair, nose up, hold it there, hold it. I felt a slight swooshing as the float keels touched the water. Ah, Arthur, no need to ride with *me* anymore!

Hack's eyes finally opened as we taxied toward the dock.

"Next time," he said gruffly, "don't waste time and fuel climbing all the way to nine thousand; five thousand is plenty high enough to get across safely."

Alone on the freight and mail flights, surrounded by grandeur and fair skies, I basked in the glory of being aloft in my new career. Sometimes I slapped the empty seat on my right as enthusiasm overflowed. Like Santa Claus delivering letters, magazines, mail-order merchandise, and other bush treasures, I found welcome at each stop.

The old salmon cannery at Steamboat Bay on Noyes Island, at the edge of the open ocean, had not operated for a quarter-century, but the owner, New England Fish Company, maintained the buildings as a supply station for fishing vessels during the summer. The rest of the year, a solitary caretaker looked after things. Charlie Waters had a radio to call in his needs to the New England Fish Company office in town, which would have the order filled and delivered to our freight room. But he had trouble receiving messages; Waters was almost deaf.

Each Wednesday I deposited his mail and cargo in a large wooden box on a float behind the cannery complex and picked up his outgoing mail there. Waters couldn't hear the airplane come in, but he checked the box periodically during the day if the weather appeared flyable.

Although Steamboat Bay was about a mile long, swells rolling in from the Gulf of Esquibel typically left a floatplane pilot only a few hundred yards in which to work. Land too far out and you bounced in the swells as if on a trampoline, subjecting the airplane to a terrible pounding; land too late and you risked skimming off the water and up onto the pebbly beach at the head of the bay. Sometimes the swells extended all the way to the beach, rendering a landing unsafe. Like so many destinations in Southeast, Steamboat Bay presented floatplane pilots a one-way-in, one-way-out situation with steep forested slopes on three sides.

The third week, swells kept me from landing two days in a row. The swells had diminished a little when I tried again that Friday, so this time I held my breath and plopped down. But how to contact Waters? I wasn't sure he would be expecting me, and my load included some groceries that might spoil if uncollected. I taxied in circles in front of the cannery, checking the old red buildings and docks for a sign of him each time the windshield swung through the complex. Only the seagulls moved about.

Finally, I decided to drop off his mail and freight in the box on the float, then taxi over to one of the docks and try to find him on foot. As I was unloading, the putt-putt-putt of a motor suddenly joined the screeching of the gulls and the slapping of the water against the cannery pilings. A moment later a long wooden skiff slid into view from behind a building and headed for the float.

"LOOKED FOR YOU THE PAST COUPLE OF DAYS," Waters yelled, smiling, his stringy white hair awry. I caught the boat and wrapped a line he handed me around a cleat. "I WAS PAINTING UP TO THE HOUSE AND SAW YOU CIRCLING." I noticed splotches of white paint on his halibut jacket. "NICE DAY."

"I tried to get in Wednesday and Thursday, but the swells. . ."

"I'M DEAF," he interrupted, shaking his head, still smiling. "CAN'T HEAR YOU." I handed him the mail sack and boxes of food, which he stacked on the bottom of the skiff. "YOU'RE THAT NEW FELLOW, AIN'T YOU?" I smiled and nodded my head. Waters caressed the stubble of his beard and scrutinized the upper slopes, which disappeared into gray stratus. "GONNA BE A WET SUMMER. BUT GOOD FISHING."

Eighty-three miles northeast, next to the mainland where Behm Canal looped by the north end of Revillagigedo Island, another facility also attracted fishermen. But while the old Steamboat Bay cannery served the blue-jean-clad, free-spirited men and women who fished for a living on commercial trollers and seiners, Bell Island Hot Springs Resort catered to board chairmen, bank presidents, and other such VIPs who fished for pleasure—some of whom arrived on their own or company yachts. When I began delivering mail and supplies, patches of snow still lay in the muskeg meadows that broke the forest on the island, and the resort's opening was a few weeks away.

Nestled in a small cove flanked by steep, lush slopes, the resort defied circling unless I climbed to about 1500 feet, which the clouds often did not permit. Instead, I buzzed by in front of the resort before landing and hoped owner Jim Dykes would hear the engine. If the fortyish, mustachioed Canadian national was not standing on the dock when I taxied in, I piled the freight on the dock and carried the mail sack up a long boardwalk that paralleled a stream on one side and hugged a slope on the other. I would find Dykes, his wife, and several workmen in one of the cabins or the generator shed or the lodge, painting this, installing that.

The resort's facilities included an anomaly in the Alaskan wilderness—a swimming pool, heated by water piped from a nearby natural hot spring. The Dykeses usually invited me to take a dip in the steaming pool. Being on a schedule, I'd settle instead for a fistful of cookies in the lodge before hurrying on my way.

Elderly Hal and Gertrude Clifford lived more modestly in Deep Bay, an unremarkable body of water near the mouth of west Behm Canal. Hal, seventy-seven, was a retired Alaska Fish and Game Department employee who now shuffled about on canes. The two had been married to each other for fifty-five years. Each week I carried their mail sack and whatever freight they had ordered by radio up the beach slope to the porch of their cabin.

"Won't you stay for a cup of coffee?" they would ask. Impatient to get on with my run, I refused them the first three weeks. By the fourth week, however, I had begun to feel guilty about rejecting the hospitality of the kindly old couple in their isolated retirement. Besides, I reminded myself, landlubber freight-room tasks awaited me for the rest of the day as soon as I returned to town. I could spare ten minutes.

Inside, the cabin illuminated only by light cascading through Visqueen-covered windows, I sat in a springy armchair while Gertrude placed a pot of water on the woodburning stove. Hal worked his way around furniture and piles of magazines to a bookcase, where he pulled out a photo album.

"I was a Fish and Game agent," he told me for the third time in four weeks as he shuffled back to my chair. While Hal provided commentary, I turned page after page of fading, often poorly focused snapshots—many cocked against the backing—showing various outdoor scenes of people and wildlife.

"Here you are, honey," Gertrude finally announced, handing me a mug of coffee.

Forty-five minutes had passed when I lifted back into the air, a sense of dereliction stirring in my conscience. The 180's radio was in the maintenance shop for repairs, so I was unable to notify the dispatcher of the delay. I hurried through the rest of my stops. Back in Ketchikan, chief pilot Gregerson strode up to me while I was tying up the airplane.

"Run into some trouble?" he asked. "You're an hour late. We were about to send someone out to look for you."

I was only a little more than a half-hour overdue, but I didn't argue the point. I confessed my visit with the Cliffords and mumbled something about public relations.

Gregerson shook his head. "We don't have time to dillydally with the customers. This is a business, not a social club. You pull this crap this summer and you'll screw up the whole schedule."

Humbled, I retreated to my station in the freight room, wondering if there would be a summer for me at the company. But when Gregerson sent me out on another freight flight two days later, I knew I was forgiven.

Now that I handled the controls periodically, checking in freight and toiling at dock tasks with the teenage lineboys increased the grumbling in my spirit. I ached constantly to be airborne. Each time a delivery truck pulled up outside the freight room's street door, I crossed my fingers; if a huge order came in, the regular flights might be unable to handle it all and I would get to transport the balance in the 180. But too often the freight disappeared in the cavernous baggage compartments of our larger 185s, Beavers, and Goose.

I learned to keep an eye on the accumulation in the bins and to tug Gregerson on the sleeve when it reached a level that would fill a 180. Sometimes the strategy worked. Even so, I averaged only four or five flights a week, while the line pilots logged that many a day. I would watch them land in Tongass Narrows out front, taxi in, unload their passengers, load up for another flight, and—after ducking behind the line shed to relieve themselves in the water—taxi right back out. Helping Gregerson load baggage into the Goose for a flight one day, I casually asked when I might be elevated to passenger-carrying line status.

"When we think you're ready," he answered, reaching for another bag.

And just what constitutes readiness, Mr. Chief Pilot? What tests must I pass, what homage must I pay, what gauntlet must I run?

"Be patient," Collins told me. "Work hard and smile a lot. They like you; I haven't heard any criticism. They just want to break you in slowly. It's standard operating procedure for an unseasoned pilot around here."

To speed up the process, I resorted to subterfuge. Quiet Judy Ball had joined the company as a reservationist the same week I began work in the freight room. Perhaps she felt a sympathetic kinship because we were both new; perhaps I represented a psychological replacement for her son, who had been reported missing in action in Vietnam a few years earlier. Whatever her motive, she became an ally in my campaign to join the full-time pilots on the line.

Several times a week a party would phone or radio a request for an immediate charter when no pilots were available. Sitting behind the counter in the waiting room across from the dispatcher's cubicle, Ball would eavesdrop on the discussion between the dispatcher and a member of management about how to handle the situation: Should Loud be diverted on his way back from Hydaburg to pick the party up? No, that would make him late for that charter with the bankers to Wrangell, and we can't have that. Well, maybe the Naha Bay charter could be postponed for a couple of hours to squeeze in the new charter. No, those Naha-bound people came all the way from Georgia and their flight has already been postponed once. Could Ulrich make an extra stop on his logging camp run to pick up the party? No, he already had a full load.

While the dispatcher wrinkled her brow and the management representative scratched his head, Ball would slip out from the counter and walk into the freight office to alert me. A minute later I would saunter through the waiting room with a smile, lingering by the dispatcher's cubicle if necessary until J was noticed.

"Hi. Busy day?"

None of my timely appearances produced a direct result, but they might have been indirectly effective through repetitive suggestion. On a late-April Thursday morning in my sixth week of apprenticeship, Gregerson walked up to me in the freight room, where I was placing destination stickers on a newly delivered load of groceries.

"Two passengers got bumped off the ten o'clock sked to Craig," he said. "I want you to take them there." Before I could utter a flustered reply, he added, "Your uniform is hanging up in the pilot's lounge. You'd better hurry; you've got to take off in fifteen minutes."

I tried to look nonchalant as I strode from the building onto the dock a few minutes later, but I grinned self-consciously when several pilots chatting by the seaplane elevator saw me and catcalled.

Though I had flown passengers routinely many times in private aircraft, the realization that now I was being paid to transport people who themselves had paid for the service tempered my elation with a somber sense of responsibility. Like a brand-new father cradling his infant, I carried my first two commercial passengers gingerly. I cruised at an unnecessarily high altitude. I circled for a second look at a light shower I would have flown into unhesitatingly if alone with freight. I made an excessively conservative approach at Craig and landed a quarter-mile out from the seaplane dock.

I adhered to the same regimen with other passengers over the next few weeks (for the time being I was restricted to scheduled flights to Craig, Klawock, and Hydaburg in good weather), and such exaggerated caution cost extra minutes that occasionally made me late for the following flight. But no complaints resulted; I was in a honeymoon period. The company expected me to tread cautiously, to deport myself with humility and conservatism. A fledgling who keeps pace with seasoned pilots is guilty of recklessness, for by definition seasoning takes experience. To compensate for my lower efficiency, the dispatcher calculated a greater margin into my flight times when scheduling subsequent flights for me.

Ironically, some passengers for whom flying was a finger-crossing, white-knuckle ordeal felt so secure with my conservatism that forever afterward they loyally requested me as their pilot—even though I eventually adopted the same shortcuts in routes and methods that had accelerated their pulses with other, far more experienced pilots.

Most of our aircraft spent the night tied down on the upper dock, and we warmed up the engines there in the morning. As a lowly freight hand, I had regarded the rumbling of the Goose's and Beavers' Pratt & Whitney engines and the snarling of the Cessnas' Continentals as an irritating uproar. Now that I was a participant rather than an observer, the enveloping din in the crisp dawn air electrified me with excitement. With a little imagination I envisioned a squadron of Hellcats warming up on the deck of an aircraft carrier before a launching.

When the engines were ready for work, pinging with heat, we pushed the aircraft one by one on a dolly across the planking to the seaplane elevator for lowering to the sea-level dock. Carts of freight and baggage also rode on the elevator. Below, we emptied the carts into the baggage compartments of the airplanes, unraveled the fuel hoses, and fetched cans of oil from the line shed, all the while bantering with the lineboys and each other.

"Hey, you want to trade flights?"

"What for?"

"Mary Simpson's on my airplane. The old bag has a crush on me."

"Anybody get the weather for Cape Pole?"

"Yeah, it's pretty good; the camp said 2000 feet and five miles, light wind."

"And you believed them?"

"Goddamn it. Someone must have puked in Nine-Four Golf yesterday. It stinks in here."

"That's just your breath ricocheting off the walls."

"Okay, go get my people, Kevin."

A lineboy scrambled up the ramp, and a minute later a small group of passengers filed slowly down, gripping the railing.

Often three or four planes taxied out at the same time, as if in formation. After takeoff a couple would continue up Tongass Narrows, bound for Craig or the logging camps on the north end of Prince of Wales. Another, Hydaburg the destination, peeled off to the west over Gravina Island, and a fourth turned north up Ward Cove for points on Behm Canal or the mainland.

Still on honeymoon, I stayed behind to sip coffee and pace about the waiting room if fog or wind plagued the morning.

"I think I can handle it, Dwight. It doesn't really look that bad."

"We'll decide what you can handle," Gregerson would answer.

Some weather-bound mornings I had company in the waiting room.

I stepped around several suitcases and shopping bags to the coffee urn and poured myself another cup, then returned to the big picture window that overlooked the dock and waterfront. Through the rain-streaked glass I resumed staring in fascination at the scene outside. Huge, foaming waves and swells raged up Tongass Narrows, spray driving 100 feet or more from the crests. Every few seconds a sheet of horizontal rain whipped by, lashing and rattling the window. The floatplanes on the dock jiggled constantly in the forty-knot wind, tugging against their tie-down lines as if trying to escape. Even the big Goose danced a bit. The tonal pitch of the wind moved up and down the scale in moans and whistles with the gusts.

It was late May, and the Season, spelled with a capital "S" in the Alaskan air taxi business, was upon us. For the next four months travel demands would stay at peak level. Even a few hours of weather delays now caused backlogs that took a couple of days of extra hustling to clean up. This was the second full day of no flying due to an intense low-pressure system that had swept in from the North Pacific with high winds and heavy rain. Behind me, the waiting room was jammed with people and luggage bound for villages or camps. Some passengers had been trying since the previous morning to fly home to their families, their dogs, their chores, their livelihoods. A few had taken a ferry to destinations that were close to home, although the state had cancelled most ferry runs due to rough seas. Those for whom flying was the only alternative to swimming or hiking had idled away the hours shopping in the stores, or drinking in the bars, or sleeping in the waiting room.

The National Weather Service station on Annette Island had predicted diminishing winds this morning, prompting many absentee passengers to return to the waiting room. But weather—more so here than elsewhere—is fickle. The wind had instead increased. Now, as I glanced about the room, frustration was evident in the taut faces. There was little talking. Most people dozed or read or stared. Even the children and babies stayed sullenly silent.

Behind the reservations counter, Judy Ball read a paperback, pausing occasionally to answer the telephone and solemnly report that no, the weather still had not improved. The dispatcher's cubicle was empty; no

34

need for Peggy Acorn at the moment. She was probably sipping coffee elsewhere in the building or downtown on errands.

A blast of air suddenly tousled my hair as the door next to the picture window opened and fellow pilot Bob Ulrich stepped in, pushing hard against the door to close it. Hunched inside a dripping rain suit and hat, he shook his head and wiped the rain off his face.

"Checking the tiedown lines," he muttered. "Christ, I'm getting sick of this crap." We walked upstairs to the pilots' lounge, where the other pilots and the lineboys were playing ping-pong, darts, or cards, or reading *Playboy* from a stack of the magazines.

"Two more refugees," somebody said as we entered. "Relax while you can."

Early in the afternoon the wind finally dropped to a steady twenty knots in the Narrows, and radio reports from Prince of Wales indicated conditions were improving there, too. Gregerson took off in a Beaver with a couple of hardy passengers and a load of freight to investigate.

"It's breezy but workable," his voice crackled over the radio in the dispatcher's cubicle fifteen minutes later. "Let's get going!"

Engines throbbing. Telephones ringing. Pilots and lineboys scrambling about loading carts and pushing dolly-supported airplanes. Passengers stretching, gathering hand luggage, and standing in line at the restroom. Fuel hoses snaking across the lower dock. Suitcases, shopping bags, and mail sacks being stuffed into baggage compartments. Yells. Epithets. Passengers crowding the ramp. In the bustle someone forgot or ignored my status as a fair-weather honeymooner, and I found myself taxiing out with a full load of passengers and gear for Craig and Klawock.

An hour and a half later I taxied in, weary from the tension of battling turbulence and rain but gratified that I had completed the flight without incident. Now for a cup of coffee inside and a few congratulatory words from the management for having eased the burden, for having, at a time of severe backlog, accepted without protest a mission in weather above and beyond my level of experience.

A lineboy stood by to help dock the 185. As I stepped out I noticed a cart full of suitcases next to him.

"You've got to go right back out to Craig with another load," he said. "And I think you've got one more after that."

Thereafter, my metamorphosis from a fledgling to a real line pilot apparently complete in the eyes of the company, I flew to all destinations in all conditions suitable for the more senior pilots. Along with that privilege came equal responsibilities; unreasonably long flight times or changing the scheduled itinerary en route without notifying the dispatcher now brought reproof.

The honeymoon was over.

But not so my education, most of which continued spontaneously. Other pilots could offer tips about places and techniques, of course. Yet the bush seemed to be a world of extenuating circumstances and unpredictable situations that forced me to improvise, to learn by trial and error as I went along. No helper stood on a beach as I taxied in to point out rocks lurking just below the surface. No radar controller was stationed in a mountain pass to advise me whether it was wiser to fly over or under a certain cloud layer. No weather briefer waited in a gusty fjord to report areas of wind shear. No fancy, multibutton computer was installed in the instrument panel to calculate how long I could try a detour and still have enough fuel to retreat.

I flew by the seat of my pants, and sometimes I got spanked.

One day my itinerary called for stops at the logging camps of Port Alice and Naukati, in that order. But visibility-reducing rain and a 500-foot ceiling forced me to fly so low that I could not relate the surrounding terrain to my chart. I weaved along shorelines, through waterways, and around forested islands in the direction of Port Alice for almost two hours before finally accepting the fact that I was hopelessly lost. I was about to land, admit the situation to my passengers, and wait for an improvement in the weather when suddenly a camp appeared out of the rain a mile ahead. I squinted. Naukati!

Immensely grateful to have my bearings although fifteen miles off course, I immediately throttled back, set up an approach, and landed.

"I thought we were going to Port Alice first," one of the passengers for that camp complained as we taxied in.

"We were," I lied. "But on the way I remembered there was a Port Alice mail sack at Naukati that another pilot dropped off by mistake, so I thought I stop here first and pick it up."

A perfect excuse. I'd have to collect an outbound mail sack at Naukati anyway, and we had a Port Alice mail sack on board; no one would know that the sack I ultimately unloaded at Port Alice was not the one I had picked up at Naukati. Of course, the passenger bound for Naukati was delighted with the change in plans.

Airborne again a few minutes later with the two Port Alice passengers and two Naukati residents going to town, I managed to work my way around to the north side of Heceta Island. Now I had only to follow the shoreline to Port Alice. I had visited the camp on observation flights with other pilots and had flown there on my own several times. But local landmarks that had become familiar at higher altitudes took on perplexing features in the rain from a perspective of 500 feet. An islet surrounded by sentry-like boulders appeared prominent as I flew by. Had I noticed it on previous trips to Port Alice? Was I really on the north side of Heceta?

Up ahead, the shoreline broke at the mouth of a major indentation. I relaxed. Port Alice, after all. I turned the corner there, began a slow descent by logged-off slopes, and peered into the rain for the camp. But instead of a community of trailers and logging vehicles a couple of miles away, the windshield suddenly filled with a log raft and the empty head of a cove. What the hell! No room to turn. I yanked off the power, lowered the flaps, and flew onto the water. The airplane fell off the step about twenty-five yards from the log raft.

When my heart dropped from my throat back into my chest, I realized we were in an uninhabited cove Port Alice used for storage of log rafts about five miles east of the camp. This time I could think of no excuse.

"Guess I made a wrong turn. Sorry about that," I said to my passengers as I taxied around to take off from the cove. All long-time loggers, they settled back into their seats, glaring at me.

OF PASSENGERS
AND PLACES

I knew nothing about logging before moving to Ketchikan. Now, after several months of flying floatplanes to logging camps and chatting with loggers both in the air and on the ground, my vocabulary blossomed with new terms: "I hear your bullbuck had to stop a fight between a couple of choker setters over a pair of corks during hoothowling last night."

But the conversations also extended beyond life within the camps and woods. With one cheek bulging from a chaw of Skoal, the loggers offered their opinion on which team would win the National League pennant, the best caliber for deer, why the Russians could not be trusted, and other matters.

Many were fascinated with the airplane and asked about the function of this or that instrument.

On one issue the loggers were in unanimous agreement. Environmental groups such as the Sierra Club had successfully sued in federal courts to prevent logging in some of the more scenic or ecologically sensitive areas. And the groups' lobbying had spurred the Forest Service into imposing additional restrictions on logging practices. Pointing out that timber is a renewable resource and that logging boosts Southeast's economy, the camp people continually blasted "those goddamn environmentalists."

In Ketchikan, where a pulp mill was the town's largest employer, many car bumpers displayed anti-environmentalist stickers. "Let the bastards freeze in the dark" was a favorite.

Although I realized logging provided considerable business for the company, I frowned at the ugly clearcuts that had denuded thousands of acres on Prince of Wales and some other islands. (The thick Southeast forest defied large-scale selective cutting, so all trees were removed within areas designated for logging.) I supported efforts to preserve untouched parts of Southeast and surreptitiously joined the Tongass Conservation Society, whose members enjoyed the popularity of Christians in the Roman Empire. One TCS president was fired from his air taxi dispatching job because of bad publicity; he complained to the Ketchikan *Daily News*, and the Associated Press and *The Wall Street Journal* ultimately picked up the story.

I was no martyr, however, so among the camp people I diplomatically kept my mouth shut when the conversation got around to "those goddamn environmentalists."

Commercial fishermen also wore beards and suspenders and chewed tobacco. But as a group the fishermen emitted a subtle sort of bush civility. While the logger's words often grated with red-neck prejudice, the fisherman's echoed quiet philosophy. The logger cussed the flies and the devil's club in the forest; the fisherman spoke of the smell and the lilt of the sea. The logger's face reflected the hard lines of a seasoned infantryman, the fisherman's the weathered features of a farmer.

Like most pilots, I kept a camera loaded with color film by my seat and welcomed flights to fishing boats for the photogenic scenery at the destinations. But while the stark clearcuts, muddy roads, and aluminum trailers of a logging camp at least stayed in the same place, the fisherman's peripatetic home was often hard to find, a speck in a world of islands and waterways.

"We're in the second bight on the south side of Ingraham Bay; you can't miss us," a skipper would radio to the dispatcher, neglecting to mention that adjacent islets hid his seiner from a lateral view and that the pilot would have to be almost directly overhead to spot it. During special fishing openings in specific locations, several dozen gilnetters might be clustered in a cove. The *Stephanie* is white with black trim? Fine, except that an airplane cannot circle low enough in the steeply sloped cove to pick out names, and there must be six or seven white gilnetters with black trim in the crowd. With fishermen moving about performing chores on most decks, waving arms are inconspicuous. Finally, with a sigh, you land, taxi amid the vessels, shut off the engine, step out on the float, and cup your hands at crewmen on a random boat:

"Where's the *Stephanie?*"

Sometimes finding the right boat was the easy part. Logging camps offered secure bumper-equipped seaplane docks in relatively sheltered waters, but a fishing boat anchored frequently in places no one had ever flown to, places with ocean swells and unmarked reefs. Not all obstructions were visible from the air. I learned to scout my proposed landing stretch for kelp patches, which often grew around marine rocks, and for the little whirlpool disturbances that revealed a slightly submerged rock or reef.

When the airplane arrived, a larger boat usually dispatched a skiff to deliver or pick up the passenger and his dufflebag, and I simply shut off the engine and waited for it to pull up alongside. Lowering a skiff was inconvenient for a smaller boat such as a troller, however. Instead, I taxied at slow idle toward the stern or the lowest point along a side, turning off the engine to drift the last few yards. I tossed the mooring lines on the floats to the outstretched hands of the crew, and they tied off the airplane—nice and tight, thank you, so the wind won't swing a wing into the vessel. My passenger climbed up to the deck—or, if outbound, stepped down to the float. Then, the lines untied, I let the plane drift away or paddled it backwards until I had maneuvering room to fire up and return to the air.

Once on board, both loggers and fishermen became able right-seat copilots. Fit and agile, accustomed to working outdoors at potentially hazardous tasks, they hesitated not a second to unfasten their seatbelts, open the door, and lean out to help me watch for rocks as we taxied to a beach to wait out the fog. If the location of a dock and the direction of the wind required coming in on the right side of the airplane, they stepped out to tie up. Under those conditions with a tourist or unathletic passenger in the right seat, I had to scramble out my side and duckwaddle across the forward spreader bar connecting the floats—sometimes bashing my head against the hot exhaust stack, sometimes slipping on oil that had dripped from the engine. Often the wind or current drifted the plane away from the dock before I could reach it. Then I had to pull the paddle from its sheath on the float and paddle in.

Most veteran fishermen, and some loggers, knew the waterways better than I. In low visibility their presence was more valuable than a radar set: "No, no, don't turn yet; the inlet's another half-mile after the next point."

As the spring days lengthened into summer, other passengers came in endless variety: contractors, tourists, students, clergymen, state troopers, sport fishermen, writers, Forest Service workers . . . Like the loggers and fishermen, many chatted above the engine roar about their businesses and purposes as we droned through the sky. I felt no envy of airline pilots who worked in front of the locked doors of jet cockpits.

Some passengers, however, made me squirm. Businessmen from the Lower Forty-eight chartered us from time to time to inspect property out in the bush they owned or wanted to evaluate. Dressed in suits, carrying briefcases, their hair trimmed and combed, they were accustomed to business jets and professional, subservient pampering. I felt like a blue-collar hick with them on board, and I imagined their critical eyes watching everything I did.

My discomfort was unwarranted. Because executives had few opportunities to travel in bush planes, they were unqualified to judge my performance. Unseasoned passengers are oblivious to a pilot's course wanderings, improper power settings, and uncoordinated turns. Loggers and fishermen, on the other hand, had earned the right to compare individual pilots, although their casual dress, banter, and nonchalance let me relax in my relative inexperience.

Like the businessmen, a mother and her infant on board occupied my constant attention. But while the businessmen caused self-consciousness, the mother and infant caused paternalism. Gone was a sense of obligation to the company to complete the trip quickly, to get back to town for my next assignment. Instead, I would detour five miles or more to pass through smoother air and give the pair a better ride. I would twist around in my seat to look at them again and again to assure they were comfortable. I would land in a slough 300 yards from the dock because the water there was calm, even though landing in rougher water closer in would have avoided a long taxi.

Most of the new mothers were village women who were going home after flying to town a few days earlier to give birth. When the scheduling coincidentally made me the pilot both ways for the same woman, we established an unspoken bond; I was special to her in the same sense that the delivering doctor would always be special. She and her child were special to me because of the responsibility I had felt, because I had been a minor participant in a solemn event in their lives. I might not remember—or never have noted—their names, but ever afterward, when they traveled on my airplane, the mothers and I smiled at each other as if we shared a secret.

I also felt a kinship with members of the clergy, who traveled often by air to minister in the camps and villages. We shared an admiration for the grandeur and variety of the scenery, although their appreciation was spiritual and mine was romantic. If weather and time cooperated, I sometimes detoured a few miles so they could view an area I thought was especially beautiful.

"How can anyone deny Creation when they look at something like that?" a young, curly-haired Baptist minister shouted above the engine as he swept his hand at a cliff with a cascading waterfall in Rudyerd Bay one day. "How can anyone say that just happened by chance?"

Reluctant to play the devil's advocate, I opted against pointing out the geological fact that the features around us had been carved by the sluggish ramblings of glaciers in the last ice age billions of years after formation of the earth.

When bad weather blocked the scenery, the clergymen still sat calmly and confidently, rarely displaying concern. Although intellectually I realized that the piety of my passengers exacted no special treatment from the laws of physics, I somehow felt more comfortable in inclement conditions with a minister at my side.

"I thought I could expect sunshine with *you* on board," I quipped to the same minister on one rainy flight.

He chuckled and glanced out his window at the rain and clouds. "Well, my car had a lot of dust on it today."

Four Roman Catholic priests from California who spent a week at Essowah Lake on Dall Island and caught not a single fish philosophically suggested afterward that the creator had not meant life to be removed from such a beautiful spot. Many lay passengers reacted less magnanimously to fishing disappointments—or other problems.

During periods of unflyable fog or wind, the waiting room inevitably contained at least one person, often a bush resident who ought to have known better, who blamed the company for the delay. The reservationist and dispatcher served as the most convenient scapegoats, but the impatient passenger would berate a pilot, a lineboy, or a mechanic if one of them dared walk by.

"Well, I'm gonna fly with somebody else!" the passenger eventually would announce, striding out the door. Sometimes he found a heroic pilot at another air service. More often the passenger returned in a few minutes, still irritated but subdued.

Occasionally weather problems brought tears to passengers. A pilot might tell himself that the fog ahead was unsafe, that in turning back he was fulfilling his legal and moral obligations to protect his passengers. But those facts could not always allay the anguish he felt when a young native girl on her way home for summer vacation began to cry because the pilot aborted the flight.

For some passengers, the problem was *not* turning back in adverse weather. When a pilot banked sharply while straining to get through a foggy pass, he could not afford distractions like a sudden scream from a frightened passenger. Fear was contagious; soon the airplane seemed to smell of it.

Fear could also be unreasonable. A young schoolteacher at Hydaburg absolutely refused to fly except in sunny, calm air—an infrequent combination in Southeast, even in summer. One week she cancelled her reservation to fly to town three times in a row because clouds moved in or a breeze picked up. Yet she was a spunky outdoors person who owned a skiff with a small outboard and spent much of her spare time exploring in it. In Alaska more people drown than die in airplanes.

Another young woman, a resident of Metlakatla, would not get in a floatplane unless the pilot promised to fly low and slow. We tried to explain to her that an emergency at low altitude gave the pilot less time to react than one at a higher altitude, and that like a bicycle, a slow-moving airplane was less controllable than a fast-moving one. Nonetheless, she remained adamant, and we humored her as much as possible.

Some of the most anxious passengers were Lower Forty-eight tourists visiting Alaska for the first time. Accustomed to airliners, which cruised miles above the peaks, some cowered after takeoff in a floatplane. "Do you *always* fly this close to the mountains?" they asked reproachfully, eyeing modest hills a safe quarter-mile away. Others thought that because the airplane was equipped with floats, it should be flown only over water for safety—not realizing that a floatplane could no more land on any condition of water than a wheelplane could land on any condition of terrain.

I found that smiling at nervous passengers often reassured them, even if I secretly felt more like praying. I tried to remember to turn around and smile at everyone in general on each flight lest their fear go undetected behind a mask of confidence.

Fear, especially when allied with a stomach unused to bumpy air, occasionally resulted in a eruption of queasiness. We placed airsickness bags conspicuously in the pockets behind each seat, and frequent passengers routinely opened one up to hold in their laps for their children. The bags also served other purposes. On one flight I noticed a stirring behind

43

me and looked over my shoulder. A boy was peeing into an airsickness bag his mother held open for him. More than once a tobacco-chewing logger or fisherman used a bag as a spitoon.

Each pilot in the company had a different tolerance level for passengers' peccadilloes. At one extreme, chief pilot Gregerson, who threw his hat on the ground when angry at company people, never lost his patience with passengers, regardless of how late, drunk, or obnoxious they might be. At the other end, one of our pilots was quick to exchange curses or even threats with a passenger who riled him.

Like the majority, my tolerance ranged in between. When a tardy passenger finally hurried down the ramp and scrambled into the cabin to join those who had shown up on time, I smiled politely at him but withheld a greeting. When someone in the airplane lit a cigarette, I refrained from criticism or grimaces but jerked open the air vent. When a garrulous passenger talked on and on in my ear while I tried to concentrate on flying in bad weather, I grunted once in a while to acknowledge him but offered no other encouragement.

For drunks, however, I had no compromise.

In many Alaskan communities you could buy a drink or a bottle as late as 5 A.M. 365 days a year. Alaskans habitually took advantage of that liberty at a higher per capita rate than residents of any other state. They drank to alleviate loneliness, to unwind in town after weeks in the bush, to celebrate the state's easy-going atmosphere. The problem was particularly prevalent among the state's natives, who were struggling with cultural upheaval and who, some people believed, had a genetic predisposition to alcohol abuse anyway.

The FAA prohibited a commercial pilot from knowingly transporting a drunk passenger. But in Alaska solvent passengers could find a bush plane as easily as they could a drink, and if one outfit turned a drunk away, another would gladly accept his money—and likely inherit his future business. Thus, our criterion was not whether a passenger could stagger to the airplane unassisted (we helped him if he could not), but whether he was reasonably orderly. Like squalls, drunks were simply part of the job.

Given the choice, I would always have chosen the squalls. The drunk crawled into the airplane in slow motion, further delaying an already late flight. He fumbled with his seatbelt like a child with shoelaces until finally you reached over and fastened it for him. If he sat up front (he did so only if the other passengers were more soused), he poked playfully at the controls while you taxied. "Come on, letch get goin'," he mumbled. After takeoff he lit one butt after another and ignored the ashtray at his side. He babbled relentlessly in your face with whiskey-soaked breath and for emphasis jostled your arm with his elbow. When the unintelligible monologue eventually passed and he began to squirm and cross his legs, you knew what was coming next:

"Hey, partner, I jush can't hold out no more."

You were tempted to let him pee in his pants, but you would have to do the post-flight scrubbing. So, you landed on the nearest lake or waterway, shut down the engine, and opened the door. He crawled out and tinkled off the float.

While I chuckled at kids relieving themselves in airsickness bags, I refused to trust drunks with the same privilege.

A certain type of passenger never got drunk or airsick, never filled the cockpit with smoke, never caused the slightest trouble, yet was always unwelcome. The first corpse I carried was a heavy, middle-aged mechanic I had flown to Craig the day before. While working on a project, he collapsed and died. He was in a black body bag when I returned in a 185 to take him back to town. Rigor mortis had not yet set in, and the village constable and I groaned as we struggled to force the sloppy body into the cabin. It sagged into each cranny we dragged and pushed it over as if reluctant to go any further into the airplane. After takeoff I glanced over my shoulder at the bag, trying to associate the contents with the breathing, moving man I had carried the day before. I kept the engine controls at climb power after leveling off and reached Ketchikan in what may have been record time.

Some corpses had entered rigor mortis days before they traveled with me and emitted a stench despite the local mortician's injections of formaldehyde. No odor, not even of vomit or feces, destroyed an appetite more readily than that of death.

Injured and sick passengers also prompted me to cruise with high power settings, unless turbulent air caused bumps that aggravated the pain. Sometimes I was unable to minimize the bumps by throttling back or changing altitude or course, and I winced vicariously with the victim at each jolt.

My constant nightmare with passengers en route to the hospital was that weather would delay or prevent me from getting them to town in time for medical help. With such passengers I sometimes charged headlong into weather I normally would have entered hesitatingly, if at all.

One commercial fisherman who had smashed his leg on his troller was so apologetic about the blood that dripped from his dressing onto the cabin floor during the flight that he offered me a ten-dollar bill to pay for the clean-up job. I refused it.

Ironically, the passengers who caused the most stress for me in my first months as a bush pilot were not drunks or corpses or the injured, but fellow pilots. Employee benefits included free travel on our aircraft, and occasionally I dropped a peer and his family or girlfriend at a lake for an outing. He voiced no criticism, offered no advice, caused no annoyances. Yet, all pilots who fly as passengers covertly judge the left-seat occupant's every action, and with one on board I felt the self-consciousness of a speaker addressing an audience of orators.

Nonpilot passengers generally assess a pilot's competence by the smoothness of his landing, although pilots riding as passengers realize that preflight planning, engine management, weather savvy, and other factors are also important yardsticks. Still, the landing is one of the most evident skills a pilot can display to a peer. Somehow, the presence of a pilot on board my airplane always seemed to activate wind gusts that caused a bouncy landing. The fellow pilot understood, of course, but still I fumed.

That phenomenon also applied when landing where a pilot from another air service stood watching from the dock. The severity of the arrival depended on the esteem the watcher commanded: the more I hoped to impress him, the harder I bounced.

Like passengers, charters now also came in endless variety. I flew a free-lance photographer to the mainland on a balmy afternoon and circled repeatedly while he snapped the shutter again and again and again to capture just the right scenes for a magazine feature on Alaskan fjords.

I took a man who had grown up at the Mary Light Station on Mary Island back to the now-automated station, where he strolled along the grounds and beaches reliving forty-year-old memories.

A cartographer on a mapping mission had me climb to 10,000 feet, an altitude so foreign to our usual scud-running routes that I felt lightheaded there.

A state Fish and Game Department agent rode with me to count mountain goats on the mainland and check the degree of winter mortality among the animals.

I flew a retired plumber around the perimeter of Revillagigedo Island, Ketchikan's island. He had lived in the town all his life but had never gone on a tour of the island, which measured fifty-three by thirty-two miles. "I didn't realize how big it is," he commented to me afterward.

The purpose of some charters was to transport things rather than people. When the bank in Metlakatla ran low on cash, I flew a sealed bag containing $20,000 in bills to the community. I took a Beaver-load of mattresses to the Yes Bay Lodge and three fifty-five-gallon drums of kerosene to a surveying camp in Wilson Arm. I ferried a dozen buckets of abalone from a boat in Cordova Bay to Ketchikan and hauled almost 1000 pounds of textbooks to the one-room school at Neets Bay.

A black bear that persisted in raiding garbage cans in a hillside neighborhood in Ketchikan eventually earned a tranquilizer dart from a Fish and Game Department gun. A van delivered the drugged bear, all four legs bound together, to our dock, and after much sweating and cursing, six of us finally got the 250-pound animal into the Beaver I was flying that day. Three agents rode along to administer another tranquilizer in case the bruin awoke prematurely and to help unload it on a Prince of Wales beach.

Most days brought each of us at least one charter along with the scheduled flights to the villages and camps. Charters held the excitement of mail call; they often took us to places we had never visited, and they could develop suddenly with the ring of a reservationist's phone or the crackle of the dispatcher's radio: "My brother is sick up at Point Baker; can you take me there right away?" Thus, we arrived at work in the morning never knowing where the day's charters would send us, or what adventures they might bring.

Some charters involved standby time, in which we waited at the destination while the passengers went about their business. For many pilots, standby time brought an opportunity to nap in the cockpit or read a few more chapters in an interesting paperback. At a logging camp, pilots on standby typically proceeded directly to the cookhouse, off limits to loggers except during mealtimes but always open without charge to pilots. Pastry, freshly baked pies, sandwiches, cookies, fruit, salads, soda pop— the cookhouse was a glutton's delight on standby, especially when a busy schedule had allowed no time for lunch.

Camp cooks were aware of the risks inherent in bush flying. They realized pilots were their source of mail and supplies, their connection with civilization. So, in both pity and gratitude, they invariably mothered us. Some became almost obnoxious in their insistent offering of additional food after we had sated ourselves, but we dared not be rude, not to a cook.

At a village or town, a pilot on standby could wander about with his camera to explore, browsing in the shops, pausing to chat with residents, warding off the local dogs' sallies.

No standby destination was more magnetic to me than Hyder, the old mining town in the extreme eastern edge of Southeast eighty miles away. The spectacular en-route scenery alone made a visit memorable— when weather permitted a direct flight across the mainland mountains; otherwise we had to follow a circuitous water route that doubled the flight time. But it was Hyder's Old West frontier atmosphere that fascinated me.

Situated deep in the mainland, its only connection with the sea the seventy-mile-long Portland Canal, the town had a population of up to 500 during its boom years in the 1920s. But mining petered out, and now pilings jutted like tree stumps from a tidal flat where most of the false-fronted buildings once stood. The surviving buildings lay on dry land near the mouth of the Salmon River beneath towering, snowcapped cliffs and peaks—terrain so steep that in late spring and early summer a waiting pilot had an excellent chance of witnessing an avalanche. A distant rumbling, like the prolonged thundering of cannon. You scan the high slopes and cliffs for a moment. There! A wall of snow tumbles down a rock face, leaving a trail of frozen clouds.

Although a sign festooned across the unpaved main street proclaimed "Friendliest Ghost Town in Alaska," the unincorporated community was home to 80 to 100 residents (the population fluctuated). Many of them qualified as eccentric individualists for whom Hyder seemed the last stop, a sanctuary where at last they could enjoy relief from the frowning of society. Resident Tom Taggart, a bearded, bespectacled iconoclast who expressed his distrust for most institutions in frequent, vitrolic letters to the editor of the Ketchikan *Daily News*, made state history one year when he became the first candidate to run for a seat in the House of Representatives as an indigent. Taggart apparently had few friends in Hyder and failed to win there, or in any other precinct in the state.

At night the population swelled when Canadians from Hyder's only neighbor, Stewart, British Columbia (population 2000), two and a half miles to the north, crossed the border to take advantage of Alaska's liberal liquor laws and the town's lack of law enforcement. The walls in the oldest of Hyder's two bars, the Glacier Inn, were plastered with thousands of dollars in autographed paper currency of several nationalities. Look closely and you could find a few bullet holes in the walls, too; partying in Hyder was often unrestrained. So was squabbling.

The young, somber Alaska state trooper sat in the right front seat of the 185 with a warrant for the arrest of a Hyder man who had blockaded a mining road at the border. The Canadians had declared the suspect an "undesirable" and denied him the use of the road, so he had parked his truck across it. The U.S. Department of Transportation office in Hyder had contacted the troopers. A state Department of Highways worker met us at the heaad of the causeway that led to the seaplane dock, and he fidgeted with excitement.

"Boy, we're glad you're here," he said to the trooper, shaking his head. "There's just been a shooting in town; one man's dead and the other's wounded, off in the woods."

He drove us into town, where the trooper pieced together the story from residents milling about on the street. Thomas Williams allegedly had been trying to saw down a fence on a disputed right-of-way between his property and that of neighbor Richard James Shields. Shields didn't approve, and both men pulled guns. Williams took several slugs in the chest and was dead on arrival at the Stewart hospital, while Shields was hit in the neck. The trooper called for help, and an hour later a Grumman Goose arrived with more troopers. Shields, who survived his injuries, surrendered peacefully. Troopers initially charged him with first-degree murder but let him go a few weeks later when the investigation failed to determine just who had shot first.

One of the newly arrived troopers took over the case of the man who had blocked the road and, after arresting him, found he was carrying a handgun. The suspect rode back to Ketchikan in handcuffs in my 185 with that trooper.

In some way each charter to Hyder proved memorable. Descending over Portland Canal one August day, my passenger and I noticed that the typical turquoise water of the canal became increasingly carmel-colored as we approached Hyder.

"I bet Summit Lake has gone out!" exclaimed my passenger, who was returning to her home in the community after visiting her husband, an immigration officer assigned to Boundary, Alaska. Sometime between late summer and early fall every year, she explained, melting of the Salmon Glacier about fifteen miles above Hyder allowed the adjacent Summit Lake to drain suddenly into the Salmon River. The massive influx of water swept mud off the banks and for a few hours discolored the canal.

A few minutes later, when we reached Hyder, the sight of a torrent pouring out the mouth of the river confirmed that the lake had indeed "gone out." I dropped my passenger at the seaplane dock, then took off and flew up the river to investigate. The normally tranquil river had gone berserk. An ocean of water raged downstream with uprooted trees and angry waves, flooding the paralleling mining road in places, licking at it in others. At the base of the glacier an explosion of water spewed continuously out a huge tunnel.

I clicked the shutter of my camera until the film-advance lever would move no further, then turned toward Ketchikan, rich with the good fortune of having witnessed a phenomenon that occurred at an unpredictable moment just once a year.

Hyder was no ghost town, despite its greeting sign, but some destinations had better qualifications. The Southeast forest was quick to reclaim neglected development. Many erstwhile mining communities, abandoned when the market for minerals declined before World War II, had since been absorbed by nature, with little to indicate their locations from the air save stands of second-growth timber.

Pilings protruding from the water and shore usually constituted the only conspicuous remnants of former salmon canneries. Among the second-growth trees at a village Indians left with the arrival of Caucasians, you might find rotting clan poles and ground depressions where homes once stood. Most old camps, canneries, and villages lay undisturbed for months or years at a time, more from their remoteness than the fact that state and federal laws officially protected them from the scavenging of artifacts. Exploring was okay as long as you left the site undisturbed.

But the need to baby the airplane often frustrated exploring at such saltwater places. With the tide ranging up to twenty-five feet and changing about every six hours, a beached floatplane could easily go adrift on an incoming tide—or aground on an outgoing one.

The dispatcher tried to schedule charters to tide-sensitive destinations like sloughs so that the airplane would arrive when the water was creeping up the gravel and mud. Unfortunately, such timing often conflicted with the customer's schedule. Sometimes bad weather delayed takeoffs.

Arrive an hour late and the bottom looks distressingly close on the taxi in. If rocks guard the area, you stand on the bow of the float and paddle the final fifty feet around slightly submerged boulders, using the paddle blade to ward off those that suddenly appear in front, hoping you'll remember how to retrace the course on the way out.

"Chop-chop!" you tell the sport fishermen at the beach as they hand you their soggy, muddy gear. The plane loaded, you start to paddle back out. But the relentless tide has dropped the water level a few inches. And the airplane rides a lot lower now under the weight of 800 additional pounds. The float keels no longer clear rocks they skimmed over a few minutes earlier.

Desperately you paddle twenty yards down the beach to a rock-free area. You clamber in and start the engine. Sandbars nudge the keels and mud tugs at the water rudders as you struggle toward freedom. Half throttle pulls the plane through some of the stickier places. In others, the floats simply stop. Cursing, you jump out and with the paddle push the plane backwards to try a different route. The remaining channels form a confusing maze as the receding tide chokes off one after another. Then, at one dead end you find the retreat too narrow, too shallow. You're stuck.

In minutes mud banks and puddles surround the aircraft in agonizing contrast to the deep water that sparkles tantalizingly a quarter-mile away.

Three pairs of eyes stare at you solemnly. "Well," you finally announce, sticking your head in the cabin, "we might as well hike back to the beach and build a fire until the tide comes in."

You step off the float to lead the way. Instantly you sink to your knees in quivering, stinking mud. You pull yourself back up on the float, brushing your trousers with your hand.

If you and your passengers are lucky, there will be a few magazines in the seat-back pockets.

Even on an incoming tide, wading through a couple of dozen feet of water to load or unload was often necessary where a shallow slope grounded the floats offshore. Smart pilots kept hip waders in the airplane for such occasions. I found them too bulky and preferred to slip off my boots and roll up my pants if the water looked too deep. In a marginal situation, I usually took a chance and kept my boots on. Inevitably, tiptoeing in or out, I got wet feet.

Charters to saltwater beaches could be challenging in other ways. When I had to pick up a party another pilot had dropped off, that pilot or the dispatcher would tap the spot on a chart before I departed. But on-scene features the chart excluded, such as reefs uncovered at low tide, could confuse me. I circled the area. If I failed to spot my passengers, I throttled back, lowered the flaps, and flew slowly along the shoreline a few feet above the water. Sometimes even then I saw only windfall, tree trunks, and rocks. A second pass. A third.

Then, like a double image that suddenly becomes discernible in an optical illusion, people were standing on the beach, waving jackets, and I wondered why I hadn't noticed them immediately.

Parties whose occupation or recreation often took them to undeveloped bush sites—survey crews, hunters, Fish and Game agents—had learned how insignificant people look to a pilot against the wilderness. They spread some brightly colored blanket or garment in an open spot near the pickup point.

By contrast, inexperienced bush travelers like "outsiders," the name many Alaskans reserved for nonresidents, frequently lacked the sense even to come out of the woods when they heard the airplane. Assuming the pilot knew exactly where to land, they instead stayed at the campsite packing gear and cleaning up. Eventually, the sound of the airplane roaring repeatedly by alerted them to the pilot's problem, and they hurried out to the beach to wave arms and yell.

A pilot could not hear yelling from the cockpit while the engine was running, of course. But yelling was effective when, as a last resort, he landed in the area of the proposed pickup, shut off the engine, climbed onto the wings, and scanned the shoreline.

"Heyyyy, over hereeee!" a voice would echo across the water.

In rugged areas with narrow beaches, like fjords, high tide might strand exploring passengers hundreds of yards from the pickup point. Even after a pilot found the party, winds and swells could keep him from landing. All you could do then was rock the wings in a farewell gesture and hope the people had enough food and dry clothes to last until conditions improved.

Freshwater lake charters seemed sweetly uncomplicated compared with saltwater operations—more shelter from the wind, fewer rocks to taxi into, and no tide. Lakes could be inviting for other reasons, too.

BURNOUT

Manzanita Lake lay on the eastern side of Revillagigedo Island near Behm Canal, along the route a pilot would logically follow back to town after dropping off two kayakers in Walker Cove. Thus over Manzanita one sunny afternoon, I noticed a Beaver tucked into a little bight on the southern shore of the lake. Staring to see if I could identify it, I recognized the color scheme as our own. I was bewildered. I had the habit of studying the schedule each day and monitoring the company frequency en route to keep track of who was flying where; sometimes an alert pilot could suggest to the dispatcher a more efficient routing of certain flights that would happen to send him to a favorite destination.

Besides myself, I knew the only other pilot currently east of Ketchikan was Jack Newport, a curly-haired, overweight high school teacher from Oregon who came north after graduation each year to fly for us during the Season. Newport had had supplies to deliver to a group of Ketchikan men who were building a cabin on the Unuk River on the mainland. His itinerary included no stops on the return trip.

Had he encountered engine trouble? I throttled back and descended to about 800 feet. I could see no sign of Newport or anyone else on the narrow, tree-lined beach as my Cessna 185 flew by. Well, I had a flight to Craig as soon as I returned; I'd tell the dispatcher about his unscheduled stop, and if anyone began considering him overdue, the company would know where he was.

I crossed the southern shore and headed toward town over the muskeg and groves of trees that separated Manzanita from Ella Lake.

But suppose Newport was sick? He might have landed because of an attack of appendicitis or other medical problem. I banked 180 degrees and, two minutes later, touched down on Manzanita. After beaching the 185, I stepped out, walked over to the Beaver, and climbed up on the right float to peer inside.

Newport was sprawled out on the middle row of seats, his mouth open, his left arm dangling by the floor, his pot belly rising and falling rhythmically with his breathing. I yanked the door open. "Jack! Hey, Jack! Are you okay?" I shook his shoulder.

His eyes opened to stare at me for a long moment. Then they glanced about the cabin for another moment. Fully awake now, he sat up quickly as if I had kicked him. "What are you doing here?" he growled, moving toward the door.

I stepped off the float, and he followed. "I saw your Beaver here and thought you might be sick or something."

Newport shook his head, strode to the tail, and pushed the plane off the beach into the water. "No, no, no, I'm fine."

"Then what were you doing here?"

He climbed into the cockpit. "What the hell do you think I was doing, you idiot, painting my toenails? I was taking a nap." The propeller spun and the 450-horsepower engine rumbled into life. He stuck his head out the window as he taxied away and yelled, "Hey, nobody has to know about this except you and me, okay?"

Newport undoubtedly was not the only floatplane pilot who had succumbed to the combination of long working days, warm, lazy weather, and an empty airplane. In recent weeks I had often had to open the cockpit air vents and direct the flow on my face to keep from nodding off. We were now in the middle of summer, the heart of the Season, and bush flying had become a test of endurance.

During my first several months at the company, the ringing of the alarm clock each morning had brought immediate spiritual intoxication. Unless the weather was bad, I dressed with the impatient excitement of a boy about to go exploring on his grandfather's farm. Where would I fly that day, I'd wonder. What interesting people would I meet, what wild-life would I spot, what adventures would I have? Days off were endless hours of fretting about the charters I was missing.

My enthusiasm persisted well after the other, more experienced pilots had begun their seasonal griping about long hours and back-to-back flights. But now, in midsummer, the frenetic pace had finally caught up with me, too. The alarm clock these days usually brought a groan and a willingness to sell my soul to the devil for another half-hour of sleep. The anticipation returned once I was up, showered, shaved, and fed, and it flew with me most of the day.

But it waned again in late afternoon or early evening. By then I was saturated with flying. I was exhausted physically from manhandling freight and jumping in and out of the airplane, and exhausted emotionally from the challenge of the bush. I wanted to go home, to have dinner, to visit friends, to do errands. Surfeit drowns any joy. Yet, the job left little time for other interests. Whether the company, or any other Alaskan air taxi, could survive the lean winter months depended on the Season's profits. No operator was going to turn away business because a pilot wanted to play backgammon with a buddy. If it was lunchtime, a pilot could darn well munch on a sandwich in the cockpit.

Although we were limited by FAA regulation to eight hours in the air in any twenty-four-hour period, often it took twelve or fourteen hours to accumulate that much flight time. Most destinations in southeastern Alaska lay within 100 miles of base; sometimes one flight involved four or more stops over half that distance. Such time-consuming aspects of the job as loading and unloading freight and passengers, taxiing, docking, fueling, and oiling didn't count as flight time.

The FAA also restricted pilots to a maximum of fourteen hours on the job in any single day. Such limits were arbitrary. Some pilots could exceed them and still function efficiently. For most of us, efficiency and judgment deteriorated before either time was up. In the late afternoon we barreled through weather that would have caused us to circle and perhaps seek a detour in the morning, when we were fresh and wary. We were more amenable to taking off with an overload in the evening, because to argue or spend time removing some of the load would have delayed the glorious moment when we could finally shuffle toward home. Our landings tended to be rougher and unorthodox after the twenty-fifth or thirtieth of the day.

Although we regularly chided the FAA for imposing excessively conservative rules in other areas of our business, most of us would have voted for shorter legal caps on flight and duty times. Since our pay depended on flight time, we applauded the eight-hour allowance only on payday.

Each pilot was responsible for keeping track of his own hours. For months I felt guilty when I told the dispatcher, "I can't take another flight or I'll be over my limit," despite my obligation to do so. Still grateful to the company for opening the door for me, still eager to impress, I felt duty-bound to continue hustling as long as the sun remained above the horizon. Bob Reeve, Noel Wien, Harold Gillam, and other famous pioneer Alaskan bush pilots rarely paid attention to the clock in the less regulated era of the 1920s and '30s. Many flew 200 hours or more a month during the Season. Who was I to complain about a mere eight hours a day?

But I could not stifle a curse when, taxiing up to the dock in Ketchikan after what I hoped was my last landing of the day, I saw a lineboy waiting for me with a fuel hose and a pile of baggage. Another flight. Up again with the setting sun glaring through the windshield and the engine roar aggravating the ringing in my ears. Back out once more while landlubbers were ordering dessert at a restaurant or holding hands in line at the Coliseum movie theater.

At home at last, I took a shower and fixed the easiest dinner possible. Even if I had the energy for socializing, the hour was often too late. So I collapsed in bed. Sleep came instantly, like passing out after a night on the town. And, almost as quickly, came the shattering noise of the alarm clock.

Each pilot had two scheduled days off a week, two precious days in which to sleep forever and attend to overdue chores like laundry and bills. In practice, we typically had to settle for one, because business would overflow and the company would run out of duty pilots. "You'll be home again in three hours," the dispatcher would say. Never mind that a single flight might force a pilot to cancel a prearranged recreational outing that would have occupied the whole day. Most of us acquiesced anyway. It was, after all, only one flight, and to refuse once we picked up the phone seemed disloyal, uncooperative. We had fewer qualms about just not answering the phone.

During my first Season the grumbling actually inspired an attempt among the pilots to unionize—a radical action in a traditionally conservative profession. A union representative from Anchorage flew down to Ketchikan several times to provide guidance during after-work meetings, and friction between the pilots and management flared occasionally into fist-shaking, threatening incidents. After initial hesitation, I joined the organizational effort, the last pilot to do so. But my misgivings continued.

Long hours, working on days off, pressure to get the job done—were not these the customary working conditions of the trade? Wouldn't the great pioneer bush pilots have shaken their heads in disgust at our flirting with a union? Perhaps because we wore airline-type uniforms we felt we were entitled to airline-type benefits.

Yet, bush pilots no longer flew rickety, underpowered airplanes built of wood and fabric. Pilots and their craft now had to meet and maintain fairly rigid standards imposed by the FAA and insurance companies. In fact, the term "bush pilot" had been officially defunct since 1958, when Congress passed the Federal Aviation Act and the FAA coined the term "air taxi" to represent updated standards of small-airplane charter pilots. Bus drivers, truck drivers, ambulance drivers, train engineers, ship captains, and airline pilots also bore the responsibility of adhering to strict rules and standards, and all had unions. Why not bush—air taxi—pilots? Should we continue accepting long hours, working on days off, and other unpleasant aspects of our livelihood just because our predecessors had?

In the end, the campaign fizzled with the involuntary departure of the unionization ringleaders.

I noted that members of management themselves stayed on the job ten, twelve, fourteen hours a day during the Season, as did the reservationists, the dispatcher, the mechanics, and the lineboys. Like us, they too wore scowls by the end of the day.

Only reservationist Jeannie Hansen maintained a constantly cheerful attitude; her boyfriend, John Lincoln, worked at the Yes Bay fishing resort up Behm Canal, and they planned to leave soon on a grand adventure: a 300-mile kayaking/camping odyssey from Ketchikan to Skagway. Sometimes in the operations room the slight brunette would adjust her glasses, smile, and gaze wistfully out the window while the rest of us chattered around her.

Gradually I found ways to make the most efficient use of my non-flying time. Letters could be written between flights. Socks for the morning could be hand-washed during the evening shower. But what to do about exercise? I was much too tired to jog after work, and jogging on my two days off a week—if I wasn't called in to fly on them—failed to satisfy my aerobics-starved body.

One morning, flying by a logging camp on Tuxekan Island, I spotted someone running along a lonely stretch of road below. I grimaced in envy for a moment. Then an idea flashed in my mind. Several times a week I got a charter with standby time; why not use that time (which might last for hours) for running instead of casually exploring or indulging at the local cookhouse? Camps and some villages offered miles of unpaved roads. I could shower in a bunkhouse or public facility.

Thereafter I stowed my running gear in the baggage compartment of the airplane and, whenever I had at least an hour's standby time at a destination, slipped into a private place to change as soon as I moored the plane.

I quickly discovered running in the bush provided an unexpected benefit. Long accustomed to sightseeing from the cockpit, I could now enjoy the country from a ground perspective. As my shoes kicked up dust on dry days and splashed through puddles on wet ones, I saw rock striations, the network of roots in an overturned tree trunk, and other details not normally noticeable from an airplane. Free from the engine noise, I listened to the rushing of a stream, the croaking of a raven (an eerie sound in fog), and the rustling of the wind in the trees. And I savored the smells: the coniferous fragrance of the forest, the pungent odor of a tidal flat, the rubbery sweetness of skunk cabbage. Sometimes my sudden appearance around a corner startled a grazing deer. Once I nearly ran into a black bear cub.

The areas I flew over every day now seemed animated, like a photo transformed into a film clip. Such intimacy with nature, along with the exercise and the hypnotic cadence of my pace, both relaxed and refreshed me. Afterward, the rest of the day always seemed to have fewer frustrations.

Too soon, these therapeutic breaks ended. Dripping with sweat one day, I returned to find my passenger, a heavy-equipment salesman, pacing by the airplane. "Where have you been?" he snapped, glancing at his watch. "I've been waiting over an hour."

"You said you'd need a couple of hours."

"Well, the person I had to see wasn't there. I could have called on a customer over at the Shoe Inlet camp, but by the time we'd get there now it'd be too late. My whole day's wasted."

I apologized, but back in town he complained to the dispatcher anyway. The word came down to all pilots: no more leaving the vicinity of the airplane on standby. Stay available in case the passengers change their plans.

Luckily, at most settlements the cookhouse or local cafe was just a short walk from the seaplane dock.

After weeks and weeks of bush flying, I had stopped at dozens of hamlets I had never heard of while a newspaper reporter. Yet, I was able to explore only a few of them. With other flights looming on the schedule, often already late because of weather detours, I usually taxied in, dropped my passengers off or picked them up, and taxied right back out like a harried New York commuter. No time for even a quick walk around. In the air I passed secluded coves, intriguing stands of second-growth timber, long-abandoned shipwrecks, and other beckoning sights. I kept a list of those I hoped to come back to with time for investigating someday. Meanwhile, I could only look and wonder.

Many such attractions went unnoticed toward the end of the day. By then I might not have stopped even with permission from the company. The obsession of getting home increased proportionately with the number of hours I had spent on the job.

Thus, I ignored the islands and waterways slipping by around me one evening as I hurried from Wrangell to Klawock to pick up three passengers. Hunger gnawed at my stomach, and my buttocks ached from six hours in the seat of a 185. The weather yawned with a 2000-foot overcast and good visibility. There was nothing in particular to grab my attention. No reason to study the beaches on Brownson Island or the waters of Ernest Sound below. Instead, I flew along with my eyes fixed on the horizon and my mind in suspension.

Two days later I walked into the operations room after a flight to check on my next trip. I glanced at dispatcher Acorn in her cubicle and opened my mouth to ask about it. The words faltered. Acorn's eyes were red, and tears streaked her cheeks. The corners of her mouth turned down, taut. Assistant manager Art Hack stood by her side, like a kindly grandfather.

"What happened?" I asked.

Acorn wiped her nose with a handkerchief. "An overturned kayak was found with the bodies of a man and a woman," she answered through sniffles.

"My god," I said, thinking immediately of Jeannie Hansen and her boyfriend, who had left on their Skagway adventure two days earlier. "Where?"

Hack filled in the details. A fishing boat had discovered the kayak the day before in Ernest Sound with John Lincoln's body tangled in the rigging of a makeshift sail. The crew had called the Coast Guard, and a forty-foot utility boat from Base Ketchikan had rushed to the scene. After a search, the vessel had found Jeannie Hansen's body washed up on the shore of Brownson Island.

Residents of Meyers Chuck reported the two had stopped at the fishing village before entering Ernest Sound and that the kayak appeared to be overloaded with camping gear. Residents also noticed that the kayak looked unstable with the crudely rigged sail. Apparently swells in the sound had capsized the kayak. Friends had already identified the bodies.

"What time did the accident happen, Art?"

Hack shrugged. "Nobody knows for sure. Sometime the day before yesterday after they left Meyers Chuck. Those poor kids. They were so excited."

Over coffee at an adjacent restaurant, I tried to shake off the image, but it hovered around me like a mythological harpy: a woman clinging to an overturned kayak with one hand and waving for help with the other while a Cessna 185 floatplane flew blithely by.

That flight had taken place late in the evening. Hansen and Lincoln were probably already dead. Certainly they were. Lincoln, caught in the rigging under water, would have drowned immediately. Hansen probably couldn't swim and also drowned quickly. If she was a swimmer, she would have died of exposure long before she reached land. And if one or both of them had still been alive, an upside-down kayak would have looked just like a log from the air. I probably would have missed a miniscule head and waving hand in the wilderness of water and forest even if I had happened to glance at the right spot at the right instant.

I was a bush pilot, not a Coast Guard crewman. My job was to transport people, freight, and mail, not scout the country for possible emergencies. Other aircraft plied these skies, too, and mountains and clouds formed a continual obstacle course. To divert my attention from my element more than periodically was foolhardy, irresponsible. You could fill a book with the names of pilots whose aircraft had collided with other planes or flown into terrain because of inattention.

Despite my excuses, the image continued to torment me until I finally unloaded it on fellow pilot Kirk Thomas while we stood on the upper dock watching a tuna boat plowing up Tongass Narrows. He repeated my own self-defenses, and the haunting subsided somewhat. When company employees took up a collection for the Jeannie Hansen Memorial Fund, established by Hansen's alma mater, Peninsula College in Port

Angeles, Washington, I donated a twenty-dollar bill.

But each time I flew by Brownson Island thereafter, a shadow fell across my spirit. And from then on I eyed the beaches and waterways with more than blank curiosity.

WINTER

The days seemed endless, but the weeks sped by. Soon it was August, and then September. The students who had come north to work at whatever odd jobs they could find returned to college with their memories and calloused hands. The last cruise ship of the Season blared its horn and sailed back down the Inside Passage to Vancouver, Seattle, or San Francisco. Loggers and fishermen spent more time in the bars. And bush pilots began going home earlier.

Now sunset rather than flight- or duty-time limits determined the end of the day. When we bitched, the subject was usually the autumn gales. Although the volume of business gradually decreased, the nature of it stayed much the same with regular daily flights to bush communities. On the recreational charter side, however, sportsmen put away their fishing gear and came to us with guns. Their most frequent quarry was the agile mountain goat on the mainland. Chief pilot Gregerson told me I was still too inexperienced for mountain goat charters and that I would continue to make the less challenging saltwater trips. But whether because he relented without notifying me or because the dispatcher forgot about the restriction, I was occasionally assigned a hunting charter anyway.

With their sheer cliffs and steep, rocky valleys, the Coast Mountains created a natural sanctuary for goats. Only the most accomplished human mountain climbers could have gotten in by themselves from sea level. State law prohibited helicopter access to hunting grounds, and most of the lakes in the high country where goats lived were too small for a floatplane. Lakes we could work typically were tucked in bowls surrounded by vertical barricades that deflected the wind in every direction. Clouds often swirled around, obscuring part of the water and adjacent rocks.

Unless the hunters had a particular lake in mind, we first scouted the ridges and slopes to locate a band of goats. Then we looked for a lake within reasonable stalking distance.

In considering lakes, we had to think not only of getting the hunters in safely, but also of getting them back out a few days later; a heavily loaded floatplane needed much more room for takeoff than for landing. The cliffs around mountain lakes usually deprived a pilot of second thoughts, because once he flew through the notch over the outflow waterfall, he was committed to landing.

While the hunters fidgeted with excitement, I'd circle a potential lake three or four times, juggling my ability, the size of the lake, the gusts, the clouds, and the probable load at pickup time. Whatever my decision, the process left my mouth dry and my armpits wet.

I went through the same mental wrestling when fueling for the pickup. Of course, I wanted enough fuel to allow detours around bad weather and to ferry the hunters out in two loads, if necessary. But each extra gallon was another six pounds the airplane had to haul off the lake; the margin between the keels of the floats and the edges of the rocks would be meager enough even with a light load.

Not long after arriving for the pickup, I faced another period of doubt. With the airplane sitting low in the water under the weight of the hunters, their gear, and perhaps several hundred pounds of goat meat, I glanced at the towering cliffs and the narrow outflow notch and cringed. Would we—could we—get off in time?

The airplane moves forward like a reluctant jogger, slowly gaining speed, inching onto the step. The sluggish acceleration increases the flow of adrenaline in your veins. Too much of a load. Already half the lake is used up, and the rocks at the far end are not so far now. Abort, your mind screams. But the airspeed indicator has crept up to forty knots. Forty-three, forty-six, fifty. Maybe, maybe. The rocks ahead look so high, so hard. Even if the plane gets off, can it climb over them? Fifty-three, fifty-five. Come on, come, come on, fly! You turn the wheel all the way to the left in an attempt to lift one wing and break half the floats' suction on the water, hastening the takeoff. The wing begins to lift. But the rocks! Too close, too close! You yank back the throttle and fishtail with the rudders to slow down. Skidding almost sideways, the plane falls off the step so close to the rocks you can see a marmot scamper across them.

"Guess we better unload some of this weight," your shaky voice tells the hunters, who are gripping whatever is within reach.

Minutes later, en route with half the load to the nearest big lake fifteen miles away, you enter a new race: can you get back to the little lake for the rest of the load before nightfall and clouds move in?

If I knew I was scheduled to pick up goat hunters the next day, visions of the airplane exploding against a cliff would sometimes jerk me awake throughout the night.

Hunters found goat trips tough as well. Storms could keep them huddling in their tents, unable to go after the game they might have traveled thousands of miles to hunt. Weather could also force them to spend extra days on the mountain while we waited for a break to sneak in. Many hunters climbed back into the airplane cold, wet, and skunked, down to their final rations, their bodies cut and bruised from falls on slippery inclines.

One of my passengers returned in a body bag. I landed in a lake to pick up two local hunters, but only one waited on the beach. He told me his buddy had broken his neck in a fall the previous day while descending a slope after shooting a goat. He cried in the airplane on the flight back to Ketchikan. There were more tears on the dock, because the wife and the widow were standing there to greet their men. State troopers flew out in a helicopter and retrieved the body the next day.

The snow line gradually lowered in the mountains. Soon the lakes were frozen, and even the goats abandoned the windy crags, taking shelter in the timbered areas far below. Now I confronted a new, more insidious menace.

While winter keeps a firm, season-long grip on the Coast Mountains, as it does on most of Alaska, it slips in and out of the archipelago like an inept invader. The prevailing oceanic air currents that bring Southeast its notorious rainfall also keep the region mild. Even in January precipitation is more likely to fall as rain than snow at sea level. When snow does accumulate in the lower elevations, it turns to slush and puddles in a few days. Some low-level, freshwater lakes stay open all year, and even in cold snaps the temperature seldom drops below the teens. At the same moment that much of interior Alaska is shivering in bitter, sub-zero cold, Ketchikan might be dripping in mid-forties rain.

"The weather here's the same all year long; there's just more of it in winter," a fisherman once commented to me with little exaggeration.

Thus, while pilots farther north had switched from floats to skis weeks earlier, we kept on splashing down at most of the same places we had served in summer.

The company had cut back to four pilots now. Still the junior member, I had been retained because several of the more experienced ones had left to spend the winter in other pursuits. During informal chats, the remaining three counseled me about winter flying. "Watch out for snow," one said. "Spend as much time looking over your shoulder as you do straight ahead," warned another.

But to me, winter seemed little more than a nuisance. The rain was harder, the wind stronger, the clouds thicker. It took longer to get from Point A to Point B, and there were more aborted flights. In return, the short daylight hours let us leave work at 4:30 P.M. or even earlier, like normal people. Winter wasn't so bad.

All morning rain had fallen from a cold, heavy overcast. Now, as I flew down Clarence Strait with a Ketchikan-bound couple from the Tlingit Indian village of Kake, the rain began turning into brief sheets of sleet. The stratus seemed to be spitting at us, defying us to continue. I had flown through sleet often in the past few weeks, never with difficulty. But the sky looked bloated, and coming from it this precipitation brought a vague apprehension.

Had I been paying attention to the outside-air temperature gauge, attached to the cylindrical air vent on the right front of the 185's cockpit, I would have noticed that the temperature had fallen eight degrees in the past four hours, and the apprehension might have become meaningful. The Tlingit woman may have sensed the same foreboding, for now she paused in the monologue she had harangued her husband with since takeoff. Uncomfortable with the sudden human silence in the airplane, I looked over my shoulder at the passengers, sitting together in the middle seats.

"You folks going to stay in town long?"

"Till the money runs out," the woman answered. The husband laughed, and both turned to stare out their respective windows. Out the windshield, the world had grown smaller. Points and bights along both sides of the strait several miles in front were disappearing in what had become continuous sleet. I angled the 185 toward the Cleveland Peninsula side of the strait until about 100 yards separated the shoreline from the left wingtip. Now I could keep land in sight in case the visibility continued to drop.

It did. The sleet thickened, and the Kasaan Peninsula side of the strait four miles off the right wingtip faded away. On our side, the hills and slopes above 600 feet also vanished in the wet, murky slop. I pushed the wheel forward to stay under the clouds and banked toward the shoreline another few yards. The microphone was clipped to a hook on the lower part of the instrument panel. I reached for it to check conditions in Ketchikan, then noticed again the black rectangular hole in the upper panel, reminding me that N1644M's radio lay on some avionics workbench in Seattle for repairs.

If I had been able to communicate with the dispatcher, the Ketchikan Flight Service Station, or other pilots in the area, I would have turned 180 degrees and spent the night with my passengers at Meyers Chuck, the nearest settlement to our position.

Snowflakes now mingled with the sleet—big, thick, flakes the size of a quarter. More and more of them. I throttled back to slow cruise power and pulled the flap lever on the floor to the first notch to lower the flaps ten degrees. Thus far little snow had fallen to sea level in the southern part of Southeast. The flurries that had fluttered over my routes had not affected visibility much.

But in this stuff I could see only about a mile. Would it get much worse? I glanced over my shoulder to look at the weather behind us and stared into the taut faces of the Tlingit couple. Beyond them, out the rear windows, visibility remained better. Town was but a twenty-minute flight from here over an easy water route, Cleveland Peninsula offering a shoreline uninterrupted by deadend bays and coves. I could hug the beach and keep flying straight ahead until the outer neighborhoods of Ketchikan appeared. If the visibility deteriorated too much, I could simply go back the way we had come, back into the sleet and then the rain, and seek another way home from there.

But the visibility had stabilized at about three-quarters of a mile, maybe higher. The altimeter read a reasonably comfortable 500 feet. I had flown in rainfog with similar conditions. Snow was a little grayer, a little thicker looking, that's all. I pushed on.

Ship Island, actually a small, mostly barren islet, slid by off the right side. A few minutes later we passed False Island, a point with an isthmus submerged in the higher tides. Familiar, friendly faces in the gloom. The next landmark would be a tiny bight, and then, and then . . .

I shifted my attention from my memory to the shoreline. The snow had suddenly intensified, and, just as suddenly, the shoreline became a vague, ghostly, barely visible outline. I immediately descended to a few feet above the water and turned toward the shore to keep it in sight, but we were already just a couple of wingspans away and the extra yards made no difference. I pulled the throttle back and jerked the flap lever up to twenty degrees. We were barely staggering through the snow now, but slowing down was academic; the shoreline, so close I could have hit it by throwing the useless microphone out the window, continued to fade in and out of obscurity.

The swells by the rocky beach looked huge and ugly—too big to land safely in, or even crash-land in. Nor was turning around an option now. I could not, of course, execute a 180 toward the shore; we were below the treetops. And the right window showed absolutely no features beyond, just a gray wall. To turn away from the shore, to lose my precious, tenuous hold on what was left in the world to grope blindly through the snow, hoping to end up back on the shoreline heading in the opposite direction . . .

Firewalling the throttle and trying to climb through the snow on instruments would also constitute suicide. Besides the fact that N1644M, like most bush planes, lacked the gyros, navigational radios, and other equipment necessary for instrument flying, my own instrument skills were woefully rusty. Had a sandy beach been available, I would have chopped the throttle and crashed on it. But the shore, when I could see it at all, showed only rocks and reefs and swells crashing over them.

Panic welled inside as I realized there was no escape, that I could only founder helplessly on. I made no attempt to reassure the passengers with white-lie downplaying of our situation. On the edge of my seat, my nose almost touching the windshield, I moved my head constantly across the Plexiglass, as if by shifting my eyes a few inches I could gain visibility. The snow now was so thick it seemed solid; clumps of it stuck to the windshield for a moment before the relative wind and propeller blast slid them up or off to the side. The airplane began to mush, and without looking—I dared not spare a second for a glance—I knew snow was accumulating on the leading edges of the wings, slowly robbing the aircraft of lift. I added a little power and the mushing ceased.

With forward visibility virtually nil, I began straining to see the shoreline out the side window. Here and there I saw a bight, a reef, a jumble of driftwood, just enough to keep the wings level. A new danger suddenly occurred to me. We were approaching Caamano Point, the lower end of Cleveland Peninsula. Between it and Point Higgins on Revillagigedo Island was the mouth of Behm Canal. How could I cross six and a half miles of open water without a land reference? With no forward visibility, how could I avoid flying right into Point Higgins, or wherever we ended up on the other side, if we reached the other side?

In desperation I decided instead to turn north at Caamano Point and follow the West Behm Canal shoreline. I had never followed that shoreline in poor visibility, although I knew from flying up and down the canal itself that it was indented with many coves and bays, all of which ended in rocks and trees. Yet, I had no other option; perhaps one of the coves or bays would provide water calm enough to plop down in before I flew into the rocks and trees.

The faint image of a Coast Guard navigational beacon appeared for a moment out the side window and faded into the snow. Caamano Point lay just ahead. I stared for the point, cautioning myself not to turn prematurely. But on and on ran the ghostly parade of rocks and driftwood like fuzzy scenes before severely myopic eyes. Where was the point? At a mere highway airspeed, the scenes passed much slower than usual. Nonetheless, the point seemed overdue.

The shoreline faded again and I strained to pick it up. Seconds passed. Suddenly I realized we were surrounded by shrouds of snow on all sides. The point had slipped by unnoticed in the snow. New adrenaline exploding into my stomach, I started to turn in panic but leveled the wings immediately, realizing the opportunity was gone. To pick up the Behm Canal shoreline now, after the 185 had traveled 200 yards or more away from land, would entail a steep bank, which, so close to the water in such limited visibility, would certainly prove fatal. The water was still too rough for a landing.

The very waves that denied us sanctuary, however, became our lifeline, for the turmoil below created enough definition to distinguish the water from the snow; I was able to maintain a sense of balance by looking down.

But how to keep from flying into land ahead? An imaginary extension of the Cleveland Peninsula shoreline, I knew, would lead to Point Higgins. I chanced a quick glance at the compass, fastened to the windshield divider above the instrument panel. One hundred twenty degrees. How much, and in which direction, had the airplane turned since we lost our grip on land at Caamano Point? Tongass Narrows ran just south of Point Higgins. If the nose was still pointing in the same direction as it had been along Cleveland Peninsula and I turned slightly to the south and held that heading, we might enter the Narrows instead of flying into land. Water in the Narrows would be sheltered enough to allow a landing. Using the rudder pedals alone to keep the wings level to avoid catching a wingtip, I turned until the compass read 125.

A glance at the airspeed indicator. Sixty-five knots. Now the panel clock: 2:34. We had already flown about a half-mile across the mouth of Behm Canal, I estimated. Six miles to go. How long would it take to fly that distance at that speed? My heart booming from fear and tension, I pulled the formula "distance equals rate times time" from ancient school days and grappled unsuccessfully with it for a moment before realizing that against the headwind our groundspeed was about sixty knots—a neat mile a minute. Two-thirty-four plus six. At 2:40 on the clock we should enter Tongass Narrows. Or suddenly encounter Point Higgins or other land, if my dead reckoning was faulty.

Flying across water out of sight of land typically creates both an illusion and a delusion for a pilot under pressure. First, he gradually suffers a form of vertigo in which the compass seems to malfunction. He has learned from flight training and experience to trust his instruments rather than his instincts, because the latter often lie while the former rarely do. So he religiously adheres to the compass heading that he intellectually knows will lead to a specific spot on the far shore.

Yet, as he plies his way across the water his instincts become increasingly insistent that the destination lies to the right or left. Sometimes changing swell patterns or wave intensities create such vertigo. Sometimes it happens in stable conditions, without apparent cause. Guided by the pilot's subconscious motor input, the airplane continually strays from the prescribed compass heading in the direction of the illusion. Again and again the pilot dutifully turns back to the heading, suspecting that in doing so he'll arrive miles off course. But if he chose the correct heading in the first place, the airplane eventually reaches the target.

Meanwhile, without landmarks by which to visually measure progress, time seems suspended. A minute becomes four, four eight or ten. The clock has obviously broken down.

Both phenomena plagued me as N1644M plowed through the snow

across the mouth of Behm Canal. The airplane wanted to fly south-southeast at about 150 degrees, which seemed to put Tongass Narrows right on the nose. I corrected repeatedly to 125, surely the wrong course, too far north, surely one more mistake on top of all the others on this flight. Darting from the water to the compass, my eyes paused for a millisecond on the clock before returning to the water. The wrinkles in my brow deepened. We had been flying forever across the mouth of Behm Canal, yet the clock read 2:36. I twirled the knob on the clock for the second time and again found it to be fully wound.

Long before six minutes had elapsed I began peering impatiently, hopefully, out the windshield for a moment when I raised my eyes to check the heading and time. The snow had lightened somewhat, and a few yards visibility had returned—a welcome margin compared with zero, although still far below a safe level. But those precious yards showed only snow each time I squinted into them.

Now, at last, the clock's hands pointed at 2:40. Still nothing. Fearful of trees suddenly looming out of the snow, I reduced power slightly to slow the aircraft further; it began to mush and I hurriedly pushed the throttle back to its former position. With snow clinging to the leading edges we were already as slow as flight allowed. On impulse I flicked on the landing lights, which merely intensified the snow. I flicked the lights off.

As the seconds passed I began to long for trees, rocks, anything. Had I turned too far south, were we flying down Clarence Strait toward the vastness of Dixon Entrance? Had we entered a Twilight Zone in which the entire world had become snow and choppy water? I opened the air vent on my face as claustrophobia began smothering me.

A light flashed ahead. I stared, holding my breath. A light flashed again. A rocky islet with a lighthouse suddenly slipped by in the snow off the right wing, and I instinctively banked away. Guard Island! A once-manned, now automated Coast Guard light station, Guard Island lay a half mile off Vallenar Point near the mouth of Tongass Narrows. Like all Ketchikan pilots, I practically worshipped Guard Island, for it served as the principal landmark for planes crossing Clarence Strait from Prince of Wales Island in low visibility. How many times I had welcomed the sight of that blinking light after a foggy crossing. Now, from a different direction, Guard Island had again shown me the way home, a fortuitous Saint Bernard.

"We're almost there!" I yelled, overwhelmed by gratitude and hope. From the corner of my eye I noticed a hand clutch the top of the seat next to me as one of my passengers leaned forward to look out the windshield. I had planned to land the second the water began to calm. But visibility increased to a quarter mile when we entered the Narrows, and I instead flew on. Now I could clearly see the shoreline on the Gravina Island side. I felt rich with the luxury of life and the comfort of encouragement. Normally, I would never have attempted flight with a mere quarter-mile visibility, nor even a half mile. But now, a whole quarter mile! We passed the Ketchikan Airport, and ahead I could see the town's waterfront.

The trembling started while we taxied toward the company dock. My entire body quivered as if with delirium tremens, and I noticed my mouth was so dry I could scarcely move my tongue. Feeling the need to make some comment to the Kake couple, I turned around.

"Well, I think we're here," I croaked.

Both passengers smiled wearily. "How did you see through that?" the woman asked. "I didn't see nothing."

The company was astonished to see me. The blizzard had moved in from the southeast hours earlier and no one had flown in or out of Ketchikan since. The airport was closed and schools were letting out early. The company assumed I had landed somewhere to wait for an improvement. No, I assured everyone, the fact that I had returned did not mean the weather was now flyable to the northwest. I had had enough visibility to sneak in, I lied, and decided to come home while I could lest the snow last several days.

There was no reprimand from the company, no phone call from the FAA for having flown through the airport control zone without a clearance while the weather was below minimums (the specialists at the flight service station, we later learned, had heard an airplane fly by but were unable to see its registration number because of the snow). No criticism was necessary; what could have influenced my future flying more than that flight itself?

As if to punctuate the lesson, a Beaver floatplane from Juneau crashed in heavy snow on Chichagof Island a month later. The pilot and sole occupant, who was killed, followed a shoreline into the mouth of a stream. Suddenly seeing trees ahead, he apparently caught a wingtip or stalled while trying to escape. Not long afterward another float-equipped Juneau Beaver disappeared in Chatham Strait in thick snow on a flight from Tenakee to Juneau. Searchers found a crumpled float, and weeks later the body of the pilot washed ashore in northern Southeast. Nothing was ever found of the rest of the plane or the four passengers.

For weeks after my ordeal in snow I was leery of flying in any condition of low visibility. Gradually, I rediscovered that fog and rain, unlike snow, changed slowly enough to allow a pilot to consider—and reconsider—the situation. In rain or sleet I looked at the outside-air temperature gauge continually and formulated some escape plan when the temperature approached the low thirties.

Snow did not always develop insidiously from rain. On days when moist, cold air blew in from the southwest, snow came in clearly defined squalls, intense, dark cells with areas of good visibility, often sunshine, in between. Snow squalls brought not only zero visibility, but vicious, thirty-knot or higher gusts, and I needed no warning from the other pilots to stay away from them. Although I could see squalls easily, avoiding them proved more difficult. They had a tendency to sneak into an area, like bullies suddenly stepping out from behind garbage cans in an alley. Again and again I'd take off from a destination to return to town, flabbergasted to find a squall blocking the route, which had been clear just ten minutes earlier. Pushed by strong winds, a squall could sweep across an airplane's path before the pilot could outrun or skirt it.

I quickly adopted the habit of heading for shelter whenever surrounding snow squalls or showers threatened to engulf me. At a camp or village my passengers and I could sip coffee inside and watch the snow swirl outside. If I had to land in a bay or cove, we drifted about in the airplane with the engine off, chatting. After a while in the latter case, I usually beached the airplane so we could climb out, stretch, throw snowballs at each other, or otherwise divert ourselves.

A typical snow cell passed within an hour, lifting its curtain of gloom to startle and delight us with a soft white world instead of the familiar green of the forest. Takeoff, however, had to await sweeping the blanket of snow from the airplane. Each company plane carried a whisk broom with which to clean the floor of the day's accumulation of dirt, cigarette butts, sick-sack envelopes, and other debris, and the broom worked well for snow removal. But climbing up on the slippery wings with little to hang onto could be treacherous, especially if the airplane was drifting rather than at a beach.

If the snow was dry, a pilot could avoid that chore by allowing the powder to blow off during the takeoff. But such laziness was risky. One morning a shower forced me to land in the West Arm of Cholmondeley Sound on a flight from Hydaburg to Ketchikan. The snow seemed dry, and when the sky brightened twenty minutes later, I decided I could simply warm up the engine and take off. But we roared down the arm for nearly a mile before the 185 finally left the water, and then the airplane climbed as if it were hauling a 1000-pound overload. Obviously, part of the snow had not blown off. The remainder was altering the delicate aerodynamic design of the wings enough to rob them of much of their lift. Well, I told myself, the rest of the snow would come off momentarily, and the airplane would promptly regain its performance.

Again I was wrong. Although I held climb power all the way to town, the 185 never attained more than ninety knots of airspeed. At the dock I climbed onto the cowling to look at the wings. Five or six foot-wide sections of snow, worn smooth by air friction, still clung to the aluminum.

Later, I realized that if the snow had blown completely off one wing but not the other, the resulting aerodynamic imbalance might have caused control problems.

As winter deepened, getting rid of the night's blanket of snow, ice, or frost became a frequent preflight chore. If the morning temperature was above freezing, we placed each airplane on the elevator, lowered it until the wings were below us, and blasted the surfaces with water from a hose. But in subfreezing air such action would quickly result in a coat of ice. Instead, we resorted to muscle power with scrapers, brooms, and ropes. The ropes we draped over a wing and pulled alternately on each end to rub off the accumulation. Sometimes we needed an hour of work in the predawn chill to get the fleet ready for the first departures.

And sometimes, minutes after we finished cleaning the airplanes, a shower of snow or freezing rain moved through and replaced the accumulation, forcing us to repeat the process.

At smaller outfits with limited facilities, ice and snow also meant problems in getting passengers and cargo down a slick ramp, especially at low tide, when the ramp pointed at a steep angle. We cheated; we simply used the elevator.

Cold mornings likewise caused tough engine starting. Since an engine that had sat in the elements all night needed prodigious priming to awaken, the possibility of fire loomed. The de Havilland Beavers' carburetored, radial engines were especially hard to start when very cold, and they were prone to backfiring and igniting excess raw fuel from priming. In case a fire spread while the pilot tried to start a Beaver engine, we stationed a second pilot or lineboy with an extinguisher a few feet away.

Often these vexing gremlins left us alone. As in spring, summer, and fall, many mornings in winter showed us mere rain or drizzle, with temperatures in the high thirties or low forties. Every few weeks, however, the usual oceanic air currents retreated before a high-pressure system over Canada. Then the sky cleared, the temperature dropped into the teens, and vicious northeast winds roared down the mainland valleys to shoot across the waterways in black microbursts that often created waterspouts. The temperature differential between the air and the water was enough so that fog-like vapor wafted from the much warmer water. Such a period—without a cloud in the sky—brought the thorniest operating conditions.

We stamped our feet and wiped our gloves across our noses while loading the aircraft in the uncommon cold, which the wind aggravated to chill factors well below zero. We screamed for someone to turn off the fuel pump master switch when, having filled a tank, we released the lever on the hose nozzle and the frozen plunger failed to pop out, allowing fuel to gush over the wing, the fuselage, the dock. Even on short flights, jarring turbulence justified climbing to 6000 or 7000 feet to get above the peaks. At those altitudes the outside-air temperature gauge read fifteen or twenty below; even with the cabin heat knob pulled out to its limit, we saw our breath in the cockpit.

Destinations protected from the prevailing southeast wind became unworkable in swells driven by the northeast wind during a clear spell. Freezing spray accumulated on the tail and floats with each takeoff, the weight on the tail requiring full forward elevator trim if the payload had a rearward center of gravity. Water rudders froze in the retracted position, forcing us to shut down the engine after landing and crawl carefully along the icy float to kick them free so we could steer.

To encourage an operable water rudder system in a cold snap, we cycled the rudders several times after takeoff. Sometimes they jammed up anyway. A surer remedy was to fly with the rudders down, but even then the water rudder cables themselves sometimes froze, rendering the rudders useless.

When we could steer after landing, we sometimes found sheltered coves and harbors that had freshwater runoffs to be clogged with ice. The floats could serve as icebreakers if the ice was fairly thin, although cutting a swath made a terrible crunching and scraping noise.

The sole virtue of a clear, cold spell was the chance to gaze at the panorama of snowcapped mountains and hills so often hidden behind the persistent winter murk. But scenery was scant compensation for fighting the chill, the northeast gusts, and the ice. After a few days of a cold snap we almost cheered when the temperature finally climbed back into the thirties, the wind switched around to the southeast, and the rain and fog returned.

Besides the occasional glimpse of a snowy spectacle and short working hours, winter brought a few other advantages. Like the virtual absence of tourists. While visitors generated substantial revenue for the company and other businesses around Alaska, they created hassles for pilots. Sedentary and overweight, tourists were often unable to struggle into the airplane without a push or a pull. Then they needed help adjusting and fastening their seatbelts. In the air they badgered the pilot with inane questions ("How do the Eskimos keep their igloos from melting when it's warm like this?") and complained like spoiled children because of turbulence or rain. On summer days when several cruise ships lay anchored in port, some of us were stuck with tourists on sightseeings flights from morning to evening.

But not in winter. Then almost all passengers were resident Southeasterners, who neither needed nor expected pampering.

For most company employees, the seasonal slowdown of winter offered a chance for a month-long vacation. Our interairline agreements permitted us to travel as commercial air passengers at greatly reduced fares; in some cases only the tax applied, putting southern California, Hawaii, and even Tahiti within financial means. I flew throughout the winter. When battle fatigue finally prompted me to get away, I had more than a vacation in mind.

ESCAPE ATTEMPT

For the third time I tore the copy paper out of the typewriter, crumpled it in my fist, and threw it into the wastebasket at the side of my desk. I sighed and glanced about the newsroom. Managing editor Clinton Andrews was studying me, his elbows on his desk and his hands folded together against his jaw. When our eyes met he lowered his to a clutter of envelopes, manuscripts, and memos in front of him.

It was July and I was in my fourth month as a reporter for the Anchorage *Daily Times*. In March I had contracted a severe case of disenchantment with bush flying. The last few weeks of winter had brought unusually bad flying weather, and almost daily bouts with snow or gales had left me exhausted physically and emotionally. When the weather finally moderated with the approach of spring, the looming specter of another Season threatened to prolong the exhaustion. Once again I faced a long, frenetic summer with little time for socializing, hiking, fishing, and other activities I enjoyed. Life had more to offer than flying floatplanes, I told myself. What future did bush flying hold for me, anyway? Rungs to climb on a career ladder, promotions to strive toward? At thirty some journalists had become editors, while I was still flying drunks and greasy freight through the rain in the boondocks. If I remained a bush pilot, I would still be flying drunks and greasy freight when I turned forty—assuming the law of averages hadn't sent me into a foggy slope by then. A few bush pilots advanced by becoming air service owners, but not on flight pay and bank loans alone. Each had capital from other sources. I didn't.

Bush flying had given me a fascinating year full of color and adventure. But overindulgence in it had produced a hangover. It was time to move on.

Résumés and writing samples to newspapers in Seattle and Anchorage had resulted in an interview with Andrews of the *Times*, Alaska's largest paper. Yet now, after more than three months in the newsroom in Anchorage, disenchantment again tormented me. Day after day I sat at my desk typing stories of importance to Anchorage but which, increasingly, meant yawns to me: faulty engineering in a new office building, overcrowding in local jails, traffic jams on area highways. Once or twice a day I varied the routine by walking over to the courthouse to peruse legal documents; I had the court beat as well as general news assignments.

My present project concerned reaction to expanded benefits the Ninth Alaska Legislature had voted for the state's workman's compensation insurance program. But my mind refused to bring order to the facts, figures, and quotes scribbled in my notebook. Instead, it wandered 700 miles southeast and wondered if the rotting totem pole by the beach at the abandoned village of Old Kasaan was still standing. It worried about the health of the elderly Cliffords in their cabin in Deep Bay, and smelled Martha Fosse's freshly baked cinnamon rolls in the cookhouse at Port Alice. Thoughts of increased premiums were interrupted by images of seiners pursing their nets in a quiet inlet. The clacking of other typewriters in the newsroom faded before the throbbing of half a dozen engines in the dawn air as pilots and lineboys pulled carts of freight, mail, and baggage to the seaplane elevator.

Other interference came from daydreams of snowcapped mountains, shimmering waterways, and forested islands, for only in my imagination did I see such scenery now. My desk was in a windowless corner, and the *Times* building sat in the heart of downtown Anchorage amid a jungle of concrete. At home, my seedy, partially furnished, ground-floor apartment looked onto a house-lined street in front and a scrap-littered lot in back. Even those views had taken weeks to find.

The ongoing construction of the 800-mile-long trans-Alaska pipeline, connecting the oil-rich North Slope with the port of Valdez, had turned Anchorage into a boomtown. Every month thousands of job-hunters, entrepreneurs, prostitutes, and dreamers flooded the city, already the state's largest community and home to half of its residents. The housing market had become a rat race. Our paper had run a story about a one-room apartment—without plumbing—that had rented for $500 a month in Fairbanks, which was also booming because of the pipeline. Every afternoon before publication dozens of apartment-hunting newcomers crowded the lobby with a fistful of coins. They grabbed a paper as soon as the circulation people placed a stack on the counter from the press-room, then slapped down twenty-five cents and rushed for the nearest pay phone while tearing the paper open to the classifieds. By the time I got off work and made the rounds, each vacancy had been rented and several unsuccessful contenders stood in a group outside, commiserating.

A *Times* employee who used his position to gain an economic advantage over the public faced dismissal if caught. But I was living in the basement of a fellow reporter's house and my dog was living in a kennel. One morning I strolled into the production room, sneaked a look at that day's classified pasteups hours before publication, and memorized the phone number of a suitable new listing. Back in the newsroom, I called the landlord. Then I drove to the address and gave him a deposit.

At least the landlord allowed pets.

Feeling Andrews's eyes on me again, I forced enough concentration to type a couple of sentences. During the job interview I had assured the managing editor that, yes, I had indeed "gotten flying out of my system" and was quite "willing to give up Southeast for life in the city." But Andrews, a bespectacled, easygoing, veteran newspaperman with a southern drawl, had no doubt seen the look of homesickness on the faces of new reporters before; I doubted that my self-conscious efforts to emit enthusiasm fooled him.

I had already ceased trying to fool myself. Trouble was, the Season was half over and operators had hired all the pilots they needed weeks earlier. One evening I had called Art Hack at home, ostensibly to say hi but actually to get a feeling for my old company's pilot needs. The company had a full crew. So did the other air services I subsequently called in Ketchikan. And, I assumed, so did other air services around the state. So now I was marooned in Anchorage, sentenced to type a story about workman's compensation insurance, with further punishment to take place daily.

The buzzer on my phone sounded, and I picked up the receiver. Static on the line. Long distance.

"Hi, this is Paul Breed of Flair Air in Klawock. Heard by the grapevine that you might be interested in coming back to Southeast to fly. We're so damn busy here that neither Kirk nor I can take a day off. We could sure use an extra pilot."

As a reporter in Ketchikan I had interviewed Paul Breed when he was commander of the Coast Guard air station on Annette Island and again, after his retirement, when he started an air taxi on Prince of Wales Island. As a pilot I had often chatted with the tall, gaunt, forty-five-year-old Coast Guard Academy graduate when we met at the same places in the bush.

I had flown to Klawock many times, but when I arrived there to work for Breed later that week, the sleepy Tlingit village looked smaller than I remembered. With just 400 residents, a couple of stores, a salmon cannery, a sawmill, and no paved roads, Klawock seemed an odd place for an air taxi. But Breed had wanted his own air service in southern Southeast, and Ketchikan already had seven outfits. No air service was based on Prince of Wales, 130 miles long and 40 miles wide, the third largest island under the American flag (behind Kodiak and Hawaii). Since many flights originating in Ketchikan went to the island, Breed reasoned that establishing his business in some community there would prove profitable for him and convenient for the island's 2500 residents.

He decided on Klawock as a logical base for his Flair Air, an acronym for fishing, logging, aviation, industry, and recreation. The village lay about fifty-five miles northwest of Ketchikan on the west coast of Prince of Wales roughly at the island's midpoint along the north/south axis. An old, twenty-four-mile logging road wound along the Harris River from Klawock to the tiny settlement of Hollis on the east side of the island. Since Hollis was the terminus for the ferry that made several runs to Ketchikan each week, Klawock had a convenient surface link with town.

Klawock also had a surface link with the island's largest shopping center; the road extended from Klawock six miles to quaint little Craig, a mostly Caucasian fishing village set on an islet connected by a short causeway to Prince of Wales. With 700 residents, it featured a handful of grocery and general stores, a couple of restaurants, two bars, a bank, hotel rooms, a cold-storage plant, and a lively atmosphere. Why not base Flair Air there? Due to exposure, Craig often was unworkable in southeasterly gales while at the same moment Klawock, sheltered behind several islets, might have a breeze of just ten knots.

Flair Air, at the bottom of the foot ramp in the Klawock boat harbor, consisted of a small office cluttered with files, magazines, and paperwork, a seaplane ramp, a fuel-storage tank, and two de Havilland Beaver float-planes. Until two days before my arrival, the outfit also had a Cessna 185 on amphibious floats. On that day Breed, harried by a tight schedule and delayed by a Grumman Widgeon ahead of him in the takeoff sequence at the Ketchikan Airport, had flown all the way back to Klawock without retracting the landing gear.

"I knew something was wrong because the cruise speed was low," he admitted, "but I was tired and thinking about the next flight, and it just didn't occur to me that the gear might still be extended."

As soon as he touched down in the Klawock harbor, the sudden deceleration caused by the drag of the gear flipped the 185. Neither Breed nor his three passengers suffered injuries beyond bumps and bruises, but of course all got wet during the evacuation. A witness hurried out in a skiff to pick them up. (Ironically, the Widgeon, which had headed in the other direction from Ketchikan, also crashed and sank.)

The accident was an acute embarrassment for Breed, the first blemish on an illustrious, twenty-year, 14,000-hour military flying career. In between two tours of duty at the Kodiak Air Station on Kodiak Island in Alaska, he had served as the commander of the Coast Guard's V.I.P. unit, which was responsible for flying cabinet-level officers and other top-rank personnel all over the world. Several times Breed himself flew the Coast Guard commandant to Europe in jets. His last assignment was as commander of the Annette Air Station near Ketchikan.

Breed's three tours in Alaska included many hazardous search and rescue flights. Even as a commander, he frequently assigned himself to a mission, performing dramatic helicopter rescues of crews aboard foundering fishing vessels, sometimes at night in stormy seas. In 1967, during his second tour at Kodiak, the Air Force Daedalian Society selected him as the person who had made the greatest contributions to search and rescue missions in Alaska for the year.

His new life was a family operation, typical of the ma-and-pa air taxis across Alaska. The first year Breed did all the flying and maintenance himself, sometimes working sixteen hours a day. "This is the only job I've ever had which consumes all my energy," he told me. His wife, Betty, served as dispatcher, reservationist, and bookkeeper. An attractive woman four years older than her husband, she chain-smoked Kools and wore her hair in a pony tail. Paul Junior, eleven, a precocious youngster who attended school in Craig, earned his allowance by pumping the floats, keeping the windshields clean, and performing other tasks. Eventually,

Breed hired a Klawock woman part-time to "give Betty some time off so she could run the family." Later, he lured Kirk Thomas from my old company in Ketchikan to help with the flying and bought two Beavers. The Breeds had a house by a lagoon near the village.

Thomas and his wife, Pam, lived with their infant son in a rented house in Craig. Pam often worked in the company office.

Although I had been hired as a pilot, the small size of the outfit imposed additional duties on me, as it did on all of us. When Betty wanted to go home for an hour or use the portable latrine outside the office, and I had no immediate flight on the schedule, I moved behind the counter to answer the phone, log reservations, dispatch for Thomas or Breed, and accept payments from customers. I also handled payments in the field, working from a fifty-dollar bankroll for cash transactions. In Ketchikan, the office people had collected fares. If the Breeds needed an errand done, like giving passengers a courtesy ride in the van or picking up supplies in Craig, and I had time between flights, I did the job. Such involvement gave me a homey sense of belonging and a deeper interest in the operation's success than I had experienced in Ketchikan. And I felt more comfortable in jeans and a casual shirt than a formal uniform.

One frustration for all of us came from the Klawock phone system. The gremlins that occupied the system were experts. They often gave both our lines a busy signal when neither was in use, thwarting efforts by potential customers to contact us. Or the gremlins deactivated the ringer on our phone so that we were unaware when callers were on the other end. When they allowed callers to reach us, the gremlins frequently interjected so much static on the line that both parties had to yell to communicate, even if the other party was as close as Craig. The Breeds had a phone extension in their home to accommodate persistent customers who finally managed to get through after the office had closed. Again and again Breed complained to the phone company, and he took out an ad in the Ketchikan *Daily News* to apologize to customers for the trouble they had in contacting us. Eventually the phone company installed new equipment, and the gremlins went elsewhere.

Many of the places I flew to now were also served by the air services in Ketchikan. But our location in Klawock often gave us an advantage over the Ketchikan outfits. When the passes across the island were shrouded in fog but the weather was otherwise workable, we inherited some flights that originated and ended on this side and which the Ketchikan pilots were unable to make. We also attracted many island residents who wanted to get to town as early in the morning as possible;

we didn't have to dispatch an airplane from Ketchikan to pick them up.

The hours were as long as they had been in Ketchikan, but my greater responsibility in the operation made them more meaningful. Breed assured that Thomas and I each got two days off a week; never once were we called in to work an extra day. While he sometimes ranted at his family to vent frustration, he rarely uttered a word of reproach to either of us. He realized different pilots have different levels of skills and perception. In a small outfit idiosyncrasies quickly become apparent. I usually needed a few more minutes to complete a multi-stop flight than Thomas or Breed, probably because I was less experienced than they. On particularly frantic days Betty might fuss, but Breed did not. He was satisfied that I brought the airplanes back without incident, that I got the job done, and that passengers had no complaints. Perhaps he also remembered the lesson he had learned about haste with the 185 amphibian.

Only once did Breed let me know he disagreed with the way I had handled a problem. I took off one morning to pick up a Ketchikan radio/television manager and his party from Black Bear Lake, just ten miles east of Klawock. The lake sat in a mountain bowl surrounded by sheer slopes and jagged peaks, with a fairly narrow gap at the mouth as the only way in or out. When I arrived clouds swirled around the gap. I circled a few times, occasionally spotting the lake through holes. The lake itself looked open, so I radioed the office that I was going in.

After landing and loading my passengers and their gear, however, I realized I could no longer tell, from my position on the lake, whether holes still remained in the clouds at the gap. I would have to be in the air to have the proper angle to check conditions there. A heavy load would make the airplane less maneuverable in case I had to make a sudden, sharp turn. I explained the situation to the passengers, unloaded them and the gear, took off and squeezed out of the lake along one side of the gap. Back at Klawock, I told Breed we would have to wait for better weather to retrieve the party safely.

"Don't you think it was kind of dumb to go into the lake if you couldn't get back out with the people?" he snapped. He shook his head in disgust and strode out of the office. That afternoon, when the sun had burned away some of the clouds, he brought out the Black Bear Lake passengers himself. He ignored me until late the following day, when he suddenly began bantering as if the incident had never happened.

Despite whatever problems the day had brought, Breed almost always said "thank you" to Thomas and me as we left for home. When we quit in early evening, the Breeds occasionally invited us to dinner at their home or the Prince of Wales Lodge down the road. While the local people were cordial—they had adopted Betty into the Frog Clan—they kept to themselves, and we did not socialize with them.

I had rented an A-frame cabin in a stand of woods near the road to Hollis, about a mile and a half from Klawock. When I walked through the village to my cabin in the evening, only the dogs were outside to notice me, to bark at my squeaky boots or sniff at the salmon scales on my trousers. From the lighted, ramshackle houses scattered along the hill that bordered the unpaved main street came the sound of quiet voices or music.

Since Klawock was officially dry, area people wanting to unwind went to nearby Craig. Once a temporary camp for Indians gathering fish eggs on adjacent Fish Egg Island, Craig had two of the island's four public bars. There, fishermen and loggers gathered in their work clothes to escape the labor and frustrations of the sea or woods. On weekend nights the jumble of voices and bursts of laughter in the smoky bars became progressively more boisterous. Not wanting to compound the challenges of bush flying with a hangover, I was content to watch from the sidelines on an occasional night when no early flights were on the schedule. The sight of some passengers rubbing their bloodshot eyes and thrusting their pallid faces into the stream from the air vents was enough vicarious revelry for me.

After hectic Anchorage, Prince of Wales seemed a refuge in both environment and mind; a stroll in the woods sufficed for entertainment. Instead of hurrying home on the last flight of the day, I sometimes throttled back to absorb the spell that turned the archipelago into soft purple at dusk.

I realized that Flair Air's need for a third pilot was seasonal only, but for the time being I was willing to live one day at a time, to leave the future alone. There were moments of regret. On difficult days when rain and fog backed up the schedule, fomenting grumbles and scowls, I wondered if I had been too hasty in leaving the *Times*. Four months was a scant period in which to acclimate to a new situation. And Anchorage's boomtown turmoil would have subsided with completion of the pipeline in a couple of years. An experienced bush pilot could always find at least a summer job, but lots of experienced journalists were driving taxicabs. Maybe I should have stuck it out for twelve months to see if my attitude changed.

Then, a day or two later, the skies would clear and the mountains, islands, and waterways would sparkle in the sunshine. Flying in short sleeves, I'd see killer whales frolicking in the waves and bears lumbering along streams and bald eagles soaring over the forest. People would smile and joke. And the good fortune to be a bush pilot would justify any sacrifices.

The transience of life and opportunities was punctuated in early September when Betty, just forty-nine, suffered a near-fatal heart attack.

Too soon, the Season began ebbing and business dwindling. At the end of October I moved back to Ketchikan, expecting to winter until air services resumed hiring in the spring. But five weeks later my old outfit there offered me a flying job. It had recently undergone a change in ownership, and a personnel shuffle had left the pilot roster short. The reorganized company was smaller and leaner. Gone were the uniforms; pilots now wore typical bush garb.

When Betty died suddenly after another heart attack, Breed himself moved to Ketchikan, bought controlling interest in a large air service, and merged Flair Air with it. Competition eventually forced him out, and he resettled in California.

While pilots played musical chairs and air services underwent periodic turnovers, some things stayed constant. The ocean continued to sweep a Pandora's Box of clouds and moisture into the region. And the forest and the mountains remained as unyielding to the aircraft of one outfit as another.

PRESSURE POINTS

▲▲▲▲▲▲▲▲▲▲▲▲▲▲▲▲▲▲▲▲▲▲

Scattered puffs of scud hung in the Harris River pass like ragged balloons, the only remnants of heavy rainfog that had blocked this and other routes across Prince of Wales Island all morning. Now, in early afternoon, the rain had stopped and the associated fog had lifted into an overcast. Beneath it, visibility was good all the way to where the pass took a sharp dogleg.

During my observation flights as an apprentice, each of my teachers had cautioned me that thick clouds often collected in the dogleg portion of this pass during precipitation. Ever since, when moisture was evident in the air I had dutifully swung wide before entering the dogleg to check conditions there and gain maneuvering room for turning around, if necessary. Sometimes I had indeed found the dogleg to be blocked by thick fog. But more often there had been just a mist or isolated cloud.

My gradually maturing weather savvy now activated an alarm somewhere inside my brain: Recent rain. Lingering scud. Watch out for dogleg.

An alarm cannot prevent danger, however, only warn of it. I chose not to listen. The morning weather delay had backed up the schedule. In addition to the five people on board my Beaver who were impatient to reach Craig on the west side of the island, a family of three inbound passengers waited there hoping to sail on the ferry *Malaspina*, due to leave Ketchikan for Seattle in just over an hour. It was winter, with its short days and lousy weather. Pilots had to push a little harder in winter. Each piece of business was vital now. If the three inbound people missed their ferry, they might call the competition the next time they had to travel by air. Swinging wide at the dogleg would cost an extra thirty seconds.

So, like a racecar driver cutting corners on turns, I barreled headlong into the dogleg—and met a wall of fog.

The curtain stretched from slope to slope and apparently from surface to ceiling. It offered no holes, not even a light spot. Yet, I was too low to turn, and the stratus immediately above prevented a climb. There was no water below to land in. Now the racecar had become a locomotive committed to rails; I could only continue on.

Terror gripped me as I realized my helplessness. I throttled back, lowered the flaps, and shoved the nose toward the treetops, automatically seeking refuge at the surface, although none was evident there. If the fog indeed lay on the trees, I would have to decide instantly whether to crash-land wherever I could, or plunge into the cloud to grope blindly through the rest of the pass to Klawock Lake on the other side.

People like to think that confronted by imminent, unavoidable, violent death or injury, they will face it with teeth clenched and head held high. Stoicism can be elusive. I gripped the wheel like a vise and began chanting, "Oh god, oh god! . . ."

Suddenly, at about fifty feet above the forest, I discovered a narrow, fog-free corridor between the trees and the fog, a corridor that had been undetectable from an angle above. Klawock Lake appeared a mile ahead at the end of the dogleg.

Over the lake in open air again, I climbed back to my original altitude, trembling. How loud had been my pathetic plea? Had my passengers heard? At the seaplane dock at Craig, they stepped out of the cabin with no sign of strain on their faces. A couple of them smiled at me. Obviously, they hadn't realized how close they had come to obliteration. They had regarded our sudden descent in the dogleg as a routine maneuver, though perhaps a bit roughly handled. The pilot, they had assumed, knew the corridor was there.

After takeoff with the three inbound passengers, I turned south to try the pass from Trocadero Bay to Twelve-Mile Arm. It was wide open. As the Beaver rumbled along toward Ketchikan, I sat grim-faced, numbed, angry at myself for having been so reckless. I had surrendered caution to pressure and had nearly killed myself and five innocent people in the process. The thought of death in the fog resurrected a specter that had only recently ceased its daily haunting.

Two months earlier a thirty-six-year-old pilot for another air service in Ketchikan and four of his six Forest Service passengers had died when their Beaver crashed in fog after takeoff from the Thorne Bay logging camp on the east side of Prince of Wales. I had learned about the accident when I arrived at the camp on a charter of my own later that morning. A group of loggers and I had watched solemnly from the seaplane dock as a rescue helicopter dangled a stretcher over the wooded knoll where the crash occurred, the rapid whomp-whomp-whomp of its rotor blades puncturing the air.

The less injured of the two survivors had already been taken to the camp infirmary. After he received initial aid, an official asked me to fly him to town for hospitalization. Still in shock, with caked blood embedded in his beard and tangled hair, and blood-soaked bandages on his face, the twenty-nine-year-old man stared blankly at his feet on the flight to Ketchikan. In short, halting sentences, he told me that the floats had grazed the treetops before a wing struck a tree. One moment he was looking out the window at the fog and the next he was lying in the brush outside the wreckage, he said. I radioed the company, and an ambulance with its red light flashing was parked on the upper dock when we landed.

I had returned immediately to Thorne Bay to resume my charter. As I entered the bay I flew over the crash site and spotted the crumpled wreck by the knoll, about 100 yards from the beach. One wing had separated and lay nearby. Loggers had cut a swath through the woods to the site.

Like motorists driving more cautiously after passing the accordion-like remains of a head-on collision, the rest of us had tiptoed about the skies for the next few days as if a crash were contagious. And for weeks afterward, the tragedy had cast a pall of gloom over the Ketchikan flying community.

How close I had come this afternoon to replenishing that gloom.

A hand tapped me on the shoulder. "Pilot, are we going to get there in time?" yelled a gray-haired man with a wrinkled brow. "The ferry's due to leave in a half-hour."

"I'll do my best."

I could only speculate as to whether pressure had compelled my fallen peer to surrender his own caution at Thorne Bay, despite his far greater experience. Certainly there was no overt pressure. No air service owner would dare tell a pilot, "Joe, you got to get through, come hell or high water." That might prompt Joe to push too hard; insurance premiums were already exorbitant. But subtle, unintentional pressure to get through pervaded every air service.

Thick rainfog hangs across the mouth of the valley. Not a solid curtain, which would simplify the go/no go decision, but a misty, shroudy one, creating a marginal situation. You circle several times, squinting out the windows. Sometimes you don't know if you want to take a dip until you get your feet wet. So, you throttle bacck, lower the flaps twenty degrees, and enter. The world around you blurs. For a minute you fly down the middle of the valley, above the stream the chart calls a river, to allow a turn in either direction. But the slopes begin to fade, and you angle to the left to keep the one on that side in sight as a reference out your side window. A mile farther on, the airplane begins slicing through clumps of scud. You zigzag around them, looking over your shoulder occasionally, wondering if you could retrace your route in case you can't get through.

If you push on and make it, pride helps quiet your pounding heart and postpones concern about the return trip. If you turn back, well, everyone understands weather problems in this part of the world, where rubber boots are standard footwear. Pilots who never turn back don't live long. Much less costly to the company to abort a charter than get lost in the fog and dump a $100,000 de Havilland Beaver floatplane and six passengers into the trees. A professional pilot, even a bush pilot who flies by the seat of his pants, has certain standards and has to stick to them.

You tell yourself these things as you fly back toward town, weaving around rainy islands, following channels and shorelines. But other voices interrupt. It wasn't that bad, they say. You should have tried skimming the treetops in the valley or climbing to the base of the clouds to check for a scud-free corridor. You should have carried enough fuel to follow the shoreline all the way around the island. You should have landed in the bay at the mouth of the valley and waited for better conditions. The company hired you to fly airplanes to wherever the customers want to go; being resourceful is part of the job. The famous pioneer bush pilots would have found a way.

Some of these other voices speak with their faces. Like the dismayed, disgusted expressions of the passengers after you announce, "Sorry, folks, the weather's no good, we'll have to go back to town."

PRESSURE POINTS

Once there, you find the other voices unrelenting. The dispatcher grimaces as she studies the schedule in her cubicle. "Well, we won't be able to try again with you people until four o'clock." Two passengers acquiesce, but the other four decide to seek an earlier charter with another outfit.

The two lineboys also make faces; before the flight they hauled 300 pounds of catalogs, mail sacks, food cartons, and other cargo from the freight room to the seaplane dock for your destination. Now they have to haul it all back and redeposit it in the appropriate bin.

The company owner is astute enough to avoid frowning at you for turning around, so he chuckles. "Found a lock on the pass, huh? Well, maybe it'll be better this afternoon."

But chuckles don't compensate for the lost revenue on the flight. They don't reimburse the four departing passengers for their fares or pay for overhead like fuel and engine wear and tear. As the owner walks away, hands in pockets, you know he's filing the turnaround in his mind, where a mental computer evaluates it against previous turnarounds and the records of other pilots.

During the week before Christmas and other especially hectic periods, a turnaround often causes direct criticism, punctuated with four-letter words. After all, the bins in the freight room are overflowing with Christmas packages, and dozens of bush residents have reservations to fly to town to catch a jet for vacation spots. The winter days are only six hours long. Half the crew is on vacation. And you turned *around*?

At such times the frustrated dispatcher or lineboys are apt to snap, "Well, Joe got through!" No matter that Joe might have enjoyed the good timing to arrive when the valley was between rainfog showers. Or maybe the weather was the same and he emerged on the other side with trembling hands and cotton mouth. What counts is that he got through. You didn't. People remember.

Sometimes pressure to push on comes from Joe himself, who took off a few minutes ahead of you and now radios: "It's pretty spooky, but you can make it. You got almost a mile in most spots." Too bad he neglects to leave a yellow line behind to mark the circuitous route he followed around the scud.

Pressure to push on can also come from bush passengers, the loggers, fishermen, trappers, and others whose occupations have inured them to the elements: "Aw, hell, this ain't nothing. I've flown with ol' Joe in stuff a lot worse than this!"

You can at least count on your paycheck regardless of turnarounds.

The owner isn't going to make pay contingent on completed flights. But with a history of turnarounds, your job is less secure. If pay is by salary, you might return after a vacation to find your services are no longer needed—and that the pilot roster includes a brand-new name. If pay is by the flight hour, you might spend more and more time sipping coffee in the operations office while the dispatcher assigns flights to comrades with less seniority but fewer turnarounds.

You try to maintain your safety standards out in the bush. Of course, you don't want to fly when the terrain is barely distinguishable from the fog. You don't want to take off with a 200-pound overload or carry a babbling, chain-smoking, drooling drunk who might grab the wheel or suddenly open a door. But if you don't, someone else will. And you can't totally ignore disappointed passengers, and frustrated dispatchers, and irritated lineboys, and forced chuckles from the boss.

So the next time a marginal situation confronts you, you try a little harder. You surrender a little more of the margin.

At home at night, a forecast of bad weather the next day leaves you feeling as if you had to deliver a speech before an assembly in the morning; you'll be flying a tightrope, with pressure on one side and disaster on the other.

Then some pilot you know crashes. The man who gave you your first floatplane ride flies into a cloud-covered mountain in British Columbia. The man who gave you your second one flies into the trees on foggy Annette Island. A friend from a competitive air taxi smashes into a hillside at Twelve-Mile Arm in rainfog. A second competitor's friend goes into trees in fog at Thorne Bay. Or you yourself have a close call—another close call. Suddenly, you're reminded—again—how temporary life is, and how precious. You resolve—again—not to push so hard anymore, and if your reputation suffers, to hell with the scorners. Never more will you allow internal or external pressure to warp your better judgment.

Unfortunately, "never" is a long time.

April rainfog had plagued the flight ever since takeoff from Ketchikan an hour earlier, forcing me to grope my way around islets and up channels and shorelines. Sitka was reporting fair conditions, so I had hoped that the weather would improve by the time we got to the Chatham Strait area. But as the Cape Decision lighthouse materialized in the windshield, I cursed: Chatham Strait beyond looked gray and dingy. The water, rainfog, and ceiling were all the same color. Now we had to cross more than twenty miles of open water out of sight of land.

The long stretch across the strait between Cape Decision, on the southern end of Kuiu Island, and Cape Ommaney, on the southern end of Baranof Island, tightened my facial muscles even in good weather. The swells were usually too deep for a safe emergency landing, and the water was always too cold to survive in for more than a few minutes. In low visibility, miss Cape Ommaney by navigating too far south and the next landfall would be the continent of Asia. Cape Decision seemed aptly named.

Instinct told me to turn back. But the two bearded fishermen on board the Cessna 185 were impatient to get to Sitka, the old Russian capital of Alaska on the outside coast of Baranof. A lucrative, two-day herring fishery would begin in that area at eight o'clock the next morning, and the men had to catch a 4 A.M. sailing of the seiner *Janet W.* Fog had grounded Alaska Airlines' flights throughout Southeast, and the ferry was not scheduled to leave Ketchikan until a day after the fishery ended. A floatplane charter was their last resort. They had already paid the company the $550 fare.

Apparently noticing my hesitation, the fisherman in the right front seat leaned toward me. "Sure appreciate your flying us out," he yelled. "The next two days have got to pay the bills till we go after salmon this summer."

"Well," I yelled back, "the strait's a little marginal, but I'll take a look."

Off the right side, the white lighthouse at Cape Decision slipped by in the rain, swells exploding against its rocky base. I pulled the chart from the side pocket, unfolded it on my lap, and estimated a magnetic course of 270 degrees to Cape Ommaney. Moments later, the 185 crossed the eastern edge of the strait. With no horizon ahead, visibility seemed much lower, and I descended from 500 feet to about 200. Every few seconds I twisted my head for a glimpse of the receding Kuiu Island shoreline, trying to hold on to it as long as possible. With each glance the reefs and trees looked more ghostly. Suddenly, they were gone.

I shifted my attention to the compass and noted that a 180-degree turn to 90 degrees would take us back to Kuiu Island, if necessary. Scribbling on the chart, I computed that we would need eleven minutes to cover the twenty miles. Subtract one for the time we had already been over the strait. Ten minutes to Cape Ommaney, which meant we should be able to see the Baranof Island shoreline in about nine minutes. The clock on the panel read 1:44.

In between glances at the compass and clock, I watched the strait out my side window. The deep, undulating swells surrounding us foamed at the crests like frothing monsters snapping at the floats. Even the gigantic *China Clipper* of the 1930s would have broken apart trying to land here. Suddenly, the engine coughed.

Adrenaline prickled my skin, and I immediately banked to begin a turn back toward Kuiu. However, a quick sweep of the instrument panel showed the manifold pressure, fuel pressure, oil pressure, oil temperature, cylinder-head temperature, and tachometer gauges to be giving normal indications. I stopped the bank, no longer sure I had actually heard a cough. The engine now sounded okay. Or did it? Somehow, its steady droning sounded — different. The fishermen were looking out the windows at the swells, ignoring the engine. I sighed as I realized I had been a victim of "automatic roughness," a well-known aviation phenomenon that seems to occur only over places where a safe emergency landing is impossible. I put the nose back on 270 degrees.

1:47. On and on we cruised across the strait. In the rainfog, visibility might have been a mile or just a few hundred feet. I could not tell. With nothing but the open North Pacific Ocean on the other side of Baranof, maybe it was unwise to head directly for Cape Ommaney. I turned to 280 degrees. Better to hit the island too far north and have to fly south for a few miles to round Cape Ommaney than miss the whole thing.

1:50. Although I had decided not to begin looking for land until the alloted time had elapsed, I began squinting into the murk ahead, cheating, hoping. Nothing.

1:52. Then, finally, 1:53, the time the Baranof shoreline should appear on the horizon. I leaned against my seat belt and stared out the windshield for some indication of land. The water and rainfog retained the same gray shade.

" 'Bout time for ol' Cape Ommaney to show up, huh?" the fisherman next to me said. He, too, concentrated on the windshield, and from the corner of my eye, I noticed his companion lean over to look between the backs of our seats out the front.

1:54. Well, maybe there was a headwind, masked by the swells. Maybe the visibility was even worse than it looked. Could we have flown into Port Herbert or some other inlet on Baranof, with the shorelines on either side invisible in the rainfog? The continuing rolling, foaming swells below gave me the answer.

My hands now were leaving wet marks on the black plastic of the control wheel. I could feel dampness on my brow and in my armpits.

And damn, the engine was sounding rough again. 1:55. I pushed the wheel forward and descended to 100 feet, but the rainfog remained just as dense and gray. And empty.

We could not possibly have already flown by Cape Ommaney in the fog too far to the south. After all, I had added a margin of 10 degrees. The lubber line in the compass still bisected 28, for 280 degees, on the rotatable card. For extra insurance, I pressed the right rudder pedal and skidded the nose to 285 degrees. 1:56. Could my arithmetic have been faulty? I scribbled on the chart again, and again came up with eleven minutes to Baranof from the Kuiu shoreline, ten from the point at which I had begun counting.

My god, 1:57. I opened the air vent, but the cold stream on my face failed to dispel the sensation that I was suffocating.

"We lost, partner?" The rear-seat fisherman asked.

"No!" I barked. But my pounding heart disagreed. 1:58 now. Where *were* we? I could not have been *this* off on the time. The swells so close below looked larger than ever. The chart showed that a 90-degree turn to the right would take us to the west coast of Baranof, if I had indeed missed Cape Ommaney to the south. If for some reason we were still over Chatham Strait, the same 90-degree turn would intercept Kuiu Island. Either way, that tactic would lead to land.

I banked until the compass read 15 degrees. "We'd better turn back," I told the fishermen while leveling the wings. They sat in silence.

I ignored the clock now and alternated my scan between the windshield and the compass. At this point, I would have traded a year's pay for an automatic direction finder on the instrument panel, which could have picked up the old Coast Guard beacon back at Cape Decision or one of several stations at Sitka. But like most bush planes, this one had no navigational radios at all. Bush destinations lacked navigational aids; some didn't even have names. Navigational radios thus were dead weight in the eyes of air taxi owners.

After concentrating on a west-northwest heading for so long, the switch to north-northeast, with the associated change in the appearance of the swell pattern, created spatial disorientation. Suddenly, I was unsure of what direction we were following. The compass read 15 degrees, but that had little significance now. According to my senses, we might as well have been flying in circles. I felt an almost overwhelming urge to bank this way and that in a desperate attempt to sight land. Instead, I forced myself to resist the growing panic and to intellectually accept 15 degrees as our escape route. It just *had* to take us to land, somewhere.

The needles on the two fuel gauges wavered just above the one-quarter marks. Enough for another seventy or eighty minutes of flying, which meant we could cover at least 150 miles before the engine sputtered and died. The chart clearly showed that regardless of our current position, 150 miles at 15 degrees would put us well into the archipelago, maybe even into the mainland. Where we ended up there was unimportant. I no longer cared about reaching Sitka or getting back to Ketchikan. I was ready to land in the very first sheltered bay, cove, or lake we saw. Even a beach or muskeg meadow would do. Nobody has moved southeastern Alaska, I reminded myself. It's still there. Hold 15 degrees and you'll find it.

Unless the compass was way off. When had the compass last been checked? When, in the busy, belt-tightening world of bush flying, had anyone bothered to check the compasses of any of our aircraft? Since we normally depended on our eyes for navigation, an inaccurate compass might go unnoticed or unreported for weeks.

"Where the hell are we?" said the man in back. "We want to go to Sitka, not Japan."

"We should see land soon," I answered, noticing that my voice quivered. Although I ached to believe that comment myself, the unknown reliability of the compass planted a question mark on my 15-degree strategy. We could simply be paralleling the outside coast of Baranof. Or the inside coast. The fuel-gauge needles looked conspicuous in their incline toward the "E" marks.

I tuned the radio to 121.5 megahertz, the international mayday frequency. Maybe the Sitka Flight Service Station could hear us, wherever we were, despite our extremely low altitude. Maybe we could get a direction finder steer. Maybe the Coast Guard could launch a helicopter and somehow get a bearing on us.

"Fellows, I'm a little unsure of our position. I'm going to call for help." I picked up the microphone. "Sitka, mayday, mayday, mayday! This is Cessna three-four-seven-seven Quebec. Over." I repeated the transmission.

A broken voice crackled unintelligibly in my headphones, but I caught the word "Quebec." Someone was trying to answer me. I called a third time just as I noticed a darkish line on the horizon. Were we about to encounter zero-zero ground fog in addition to the misty rainfog? My pulse quickened.

"Land!" cried one of my passengers. I stopped breathing for a moment. The darkish line appeared to be far away, but seconds later the windshield filled with coves, crags, trees, reefs, and breaking swells. I turned to follow the shoreline and tried to correlate the features with the chart. The visibility and low altitude thwarted me, but not the fishermen.

"There's Branch Bay!" one of them said. "I've holed up in there more than once."

Branch Bay put us on the outside coast of Baranof some twelve miles northwest of Cape Ommaney. Being back in contact with land, knowing where we were—no ex-prisoner ever breathed a deeper sigh of relief at a commuted sentence.

The visibility improved as we flew up the coast, and so did the aural health of the engine. By the time we passed Crawfish Inlet we had climbed to almost 1000 feet. The radio suddenly boomed in my ears: "Cessna three-four-seven-seven Quebec, Sitka Radio, how do you read?"

"Sitka, seven-seven Quebec, loud and clear, go ahead."

"I've been trying to call you for twenty minutes," said the voice in a rapid New England twang. "Do you require assistance?"

"Negative. We had a problem for a while, but it's been resolved."

After landing in Sitka Channel, I deposited the fishermen at a downtown dock.

"Interesting ride, captain," one of them said as they shouldered their dufflebags.

I found a soda machine in a nearby building and chug-a-lugged a cola to clear the paste from my mouth. Then I rented a room in a downtown lodge for the night.

Before landing back in Ketchikan under a high overcast the next day, I checked the compass against the runway heading at the Ketchikan Airport and found it read 18 degrees too far north. No wonder I had missed Cape Ommaney to the south. I complained so bitterly at the company that in a week all our compasses had been checked and adjusted.

And I swore to others and myself that I would never again let pressure force me into a marginal situation without the proper equipment. But even as I made that pledge, I knew that "never" was a long time.

RELIEF VALVE

For the first few minutes after takeoff from Ketchikan, the man and two women sitting in the three middle seats of the Beaver chattered noisily. Occasionally an odor of whiskey wafted into the cockpit. Pilot Kirk Thomas paid little attention, however, and instead gazed at the passing peaks, coves, and forested islands. Thomas was used to merriment in the cabin, and these three had a special reason to be merry: they were en route to picturesque Petersburg to attend the Little Norway Festival. Petersburg sponsored the festival each spring to celebrate its Norwegian heritage. There were parades, banners, and brightly clad lasses, of course, but mostly the festival was a five-day orgy of parties and making whoopee—a sort of far-north Mardi Gras. Like many participants, the three Beaver passengers had begun celebrating early.

Now there was a rustling in the middle seats, and the chatter changed to whispering and muffled giggling. Suddenly, an uproarious shriek shattered Thomas's daydreaming, prompting him to look over his shoulder.

The male passenger was stark naked, wearing not even his seatbelt. He grinned and saluted the pilot with a flask while the two women squealed their delight.

This proved too much for Thomas's Mormon upbringing. "Put your clothes back on or I'll dump you on the nearest beach!" he snapped.

The man sheepishly complied. But the giggling and swigging promptly resumed, and when the trio stumbled onto the dock at Petersburg, the man stripped again, howled, and dove into the harbor. Since the water in Alaska is frigid year-round, he presumably found the experience somewhat sobering.

The incident prompted chuckles when Thomas related it to us back in Ketchikan, but the talk soon turned to other things. We were used to bizarre, humorous incidents. We could hardly have avoided them in a wilderness where we flew by the seat of our pants in direct contact with a motley assortment of people and cargo. At least in retrospect, the farcical was welcome for its therapeutic balancing of the pressure, the close calls, and the insecurities of our livelihood.

Sometimes even pilots stripped. It was late afternoon in September, and after climbing out from Ketchikan with two deer hunters bound for Josephine Lake on Prince of Wales, I noticed a vast expanse of thick ground fog boiling in from the ocean, blanketing everything in its path like lava. If the fog rolled into Ketchikan before I returned from Josephine, I would have to spend the night in the boondocks.

Cruising the Beaver at climb power saved a few minutes, and at the lake I decided to buy several more by landing immediately instead of circling first to check for debris. Once on the water, I taxied quickly into the cove where the lake's Forest Service cabin was situated.

Suddenly, the airplane stopped. I leaned out the door. Just below the surface, the floats had snagged a network of windfall, which I would have detected had I taken the time to circle. Since the beach lay just fifty feet ahead, I dared not risk trying to rock the Beaver free with power and elevator lest it suddenly surge forward. Instead, I shut down the engine, yanked the paddle out of its sheath on the float, and tried to push us off the snags. We moved not an inch. The tick-tock, tick-tock of passing time screamed louder and louder in my mind as I envisioned the fog rolling closer to town.

I knew the lake water was icy cold; on the approach I had noticed patches of old, turquoise-tinted ice from the previous winter clinging to the shore in places where the steep slopes of Copper Mountain blocked the sun. But I had no choice. Cursing in the quiet mountain air, I tore off my outer clothing and, wearing just my underwear, slipped gingerly into the waist-deep water. Moaning and gasping for breath from the chill, I was able to pull the Beaver, now 160 pounds lighter, free and tow it to shore. The hunters and I practically threw their camping gear and supplies out of the airplane.

Then, wincing again, I towed it back out beyond the logjam and climbed in. With no towel and no time to dress anyway, I left my clothes in a pile on the floor and immediately took off, shivering and dripping. The Beaver's 450-horsepower engine blasted hot air out of the cabin heater vents, and soon I was smiling like a sunbather.

The fog was rolling over the hills of Gravina Island, enveloping the fringes of the Ketchikan Airport, when I landed in Tongass Narrows. At the dock, a couple of lineboys stared at me for a moment, then cat-called and rushed off. I had already dressed when they hurried back with cameras and half a dozen pilots, passengers, and office people.

Floatplane pilots took unscheduled dips for other reasons. Beach the airplane too lightly before helping carry supplies to a cabin or camp and you might return to find an offshore wind or incoming tide had drifted it away. If a skiff was unavailable, off with your clothes and into the water. Habitually offer to carry female passengers from the airplane through the last few yards of shallow water to the beach and the law of averages guaranteed periodic stumbles on unseen rocks. And no float-plane pilot could avoid the occasional loss of balance while maneuvering the plane at the dock or stepping along the float to the cockpit.

The likelihood of an embarrassing event seemed to increase in direct proportion to the size of the audience.

Or the desire to make a positive impression. I had been a commercial bush pilot for less than three months when I returned from a flight one morning to find three attractive young women in the waiting room. College students from Washington state on vacation in Alaska, they had chartered the company for transportation to the Forest Service cabin at the lower end of Patching Lake. A busy schedule had delayed accommodating them, and the dispatcher had assured them they could go out with the next available pilot.

"Well, we won't keep you waiting a second longer," I announced in an unnecessarily loud voice. "Let's go." Five minutes later we taxied away from the dock, the rear of the 185 filled with camping gear. Patching Lake sat on Revillagigedo Island about eighteen miles north of Ketchikan, adjacent to Heckman Lake. Patching and Heckman were similar in shape, and each had a cabin on its lower end. Although I had never landed at either, I had flown by several times and felt confident I knew which was which. No need to unfold a chart and let three pretty girls think I was a new pilot. So I spent the flight instead describing the excitement and challenges of bush flying.

An axiom called Murphy's Law, applicable to all of life but especially familiar in aviation, holds that if someone can make a certain mistake, he eventually will. Since it was possible for a relatively inexperienced bush pilot to drop Patching-bound passengers off at Heckman . . .

The pilot who landed at Patching four days later to pick up the women found an empty cabin, thought about the situation, took off for Heckman, and located them there. They told the pilot they had discovered the mistake immediately from Forest Service literature inside the cabin. They had run outside and yelled and waved and jumped up and down, but I was already roaring down the lake on takeoff. Nonetheless, the women said they had enjoyed themselves, and they admitted the mistake had contributed some adventure and humor to the outing.

Ever afterward, whenever I had a lake trip, the dispatcher cheerfully reminded me not to land at Heckman — even if the destination were 100 miles in the opposite direction. If Heckman itself was the destination, I was admonished not to land at Patching.

Pilots were not always the brunt of humor in the bush. One afternoon I had three elderly men to return to the village of Hydaburg. Plastered, they sat like zombies on the couch in the waiting room, slipping a bottle back and forth among themselves. At flight time they stumbled down the ramp single file like the Three Stooges. Not wanting any of them next to me, I placed all three in the middle row of the Beaver.

The Christmas holidays were a few weeks away, and the management had decided to distribute Christmas cards imprinted with a color photo of a company airplane. Sunlight, blue sky, and scattered cumulus clouds graced the afternoon, and the hills wore a blanket of snow — perfect conditions for a photo-taking session. The Beaver I was flying had a sharp paint job in the company's scheme, and pilot Bob Ulrich was bound in the same direction as I at about the same time. So he arranged to follow me in his 185 and try for some Christmas card-quality shots.

Over the radio we agreed that the mountains in the vicinity of Cholmondeley Sound would provide the best backdrop. When we reached that area, Ulrich, who had been following out of sight, pulled alongside the Beaver and began clicking the shutter. Since he had the faster airplane, I simple maintained altitude, course, and airspeed and let him do the necessary maneuvering. From the corner of my eye I kept track of the 185's position. The three drunks had been sitting quietly in the middle seats, sharing the bottle. Suddenly, one of them recoiled as he noticed the 185 out the window on his side a mere 150 feet away. A hand gripped my shoulder.

"Airplane!" the drunk cried, spraying me with a nauseating stream of whiskey breath. "There's a airplane out there!"

At that moment my headphones boomed as Ulrich said he had what he needed, and the 185 peeled off and disappeared from view. I turned and looked out the drunk's window.

"What airplane?" I teased. "I don't see any airplane."

The drunk looked back out, his mouth agape when he saw an empty sky. I heard an unintelligible exclamation. He pressed his nose against the window and stared while his open-mouthed cronies peered over his shoulder. Then he turned to me, his eyebrows nearly touching his eyelids in a bewildered frown.

"There wush a airplane out there!" he whined.

I shook my head. "I don't see any airplane."

The drunk looked again, then grabbed the bottle from one of the others and took a long swig. I was still chuckling when we landed at the village a few minutes later.

Drunks could be much less passive than the three zombies. In men, alcohol sometimes aroused atavistic instincts that stimulated them into wrestling the pilot or trying to fly the plane, if it had dual controls. In women, alcohol could arouse amorous intentions that also incited assaults. But sobriety alone was no guarantee of a peaceful flight. We encountered continual turbulence one blustery morning on a sightseeing tour of the Ketchikan area. From the corner of my eye I noticed the three Lower Forty-eight tourists jump and grip their seats at each bump. Obviously, they were unaccustomed to flying in a small airplane. After a particularly sharp jolt, something suddenly hit me on the head. I turned around. "Stop doing that!" a middle-aged woman snapped, glaring at me, her pocketbook poised for another blow.

At least corpses behaved themselves en route—although they sometimes had trouble getting to their own funerals. After highly respected Hydaburg leader Clarence Peele died during a March visit to Ketchikan, dozens of friends and relatives from around the Pacific Northwest gathered in Ketchikan for transportation to Hydaburg for the services. On the day of the funeral, we shuttled planeload after planeload of mourners to the village. With the job finally completed late in the afternoon, it was time to deliver the casket. By then, however, rainfog had developed on Prince of Wales, and pilot Bob Mayne could not find a hole through the passes to the west side. He returned to town for the night, and Ketchikan Mortuary reclaimed the casket.

In the morning, fog still blocked the passes, so Mayne landed at Hollis on the east side of Prince of Wales with the casket to wait for the clouds to dissipate. Unable to reach Craig to pick up six schoolgirls, I also landed at Hollis. For an hour we idled at the seaplane dock in the quiet air, chatting through streams of vaporized breath. When the wall of fog hanging at the mouths of nearby Harris River and Twelve-Mile Arm showed no signs of breaking, I contacted Ketchikan on the airplane radio. The dispatcher asked me to stand by while she called Craig. A minute later she was back in my headphones to inform me that the schoolgirls were scheduled to compete in a Ketchikan basketball tournament; their coach had decided to drive them to Hollis in a van to catch the airplane there rather than wait indefinitely for better weather. The entire village of Hydaburg, the dispatcher added, was standing by for Mayne to arrive with the casket.

An hour passed. Then another. No van from Craig. I radioed the company again, and the dispatcher called Craig. That community, she reported, was mystified about the whereabouts of the van and would send a car to investigate. Meanwhile, she said, Hydaburg had sent a seiner toward Craig. The crew would borrow a truck there, drive to Hollis, pick up the casket from Mayne, and transport it to the village by boat.

By early afternoon Mayne and I had exhausted all topics of conversation, thumbed through each dogeared magazine stuffed in the aircrafts' seat pockets, and explored every yard of Hollis within a 300-yard radius of the dock. Still no vehicles. No van, no car, no truck. What was going on, we wondered? Surely we were the victims of some complex prank. Again I radioed Ketchikan; the dispatcher said the Craig state trooper would leave immediately to look for the three vehicles.

Moments later, a beam of sunlight burned through the clouds and illuminated a tidal flat across the bay. A patch of blue was visible in the break. In minutes other breaks formed, and sections of snowy ridges and hillsides appeared through the gray. We untied our Beavers, started the engines, and taxied out. When we roared off a few minutes later, only scattered remnants of fog remained. Mayne headed up Twelve-Mile Arm toward Hydaburg, and I flew into the Harris River valley, paralleling the snow-covered road to look for the missing vehicles. I quickly solved part of the mystery. The van was in a ditch about three miles from Hollis. I circled, and an adult and six girls waved. Some five miles farther on I found the car mired off the road. The lone occupant also waved when I circled.

I notified Ketchikan of the discoveries, and the dispatcher told me to continue on to Craig to pick up a different load of passengers. As I throttled back to descend I noticed a state trooper van racing along the road.

Later I learned the trooper had managed to stay on the road and had picked up all eight occupants of the two vehicles, none of whom had been hurt. The girls eventually got to Ketchikan on another company airplane, although not in time for the tournament. Mayne finally delivered the casket to Hydaburg, allowing the belated funeral to take place. By radio the village recalled the seiner, which because of thick fog had not yet reached Craig.

Fog delays could be especially notable when the passengers included dignitaries. The phone rang at Todd's Air Service late one fall afternoon. Four men in Wrangell urgently wanted to get to Ketchikan before dark, but other air services had refused to fly them because of the hour; could Todd's do it? Dixie Jewett, tall, independent, and capable, hurried down the ramp to her 185. The hills had already lost their features in dusk and rainfog when she landed in Wrangell Harbor. Minutes after takeoff, squinting to see through the gathering gloom, she realized she could no longer continue safely with passengers on board. Spotting the lights of a tugboat by Zarembo Island, Jewett felt her way onto the water, taxied up, and asked the skipper to take her passengers on into town.

The startled skipper humbly agreed when he learned they were then-Governor Bill Egan, who was on a campaign swing in Southeast; Alaska's sole congressman, Nick Begich (who would later disappear in a Cessna 310 with Louisiana congressman Hale Boggs); and two aides.

While Jewett took off for a nearby logging camp to spend the night, the tug headed for Ketchikan, delivering its distinguished guests to anxious officials hours after a scheduled dinner engagement. The incident made headlines around the state, and Jewett, the only female bush pilot in Ketchikan, endured ribbing from her male counterparts for weeks afterward.

Another mariner also received an unexpected valuable donation from the air, although he never met his benefactors. Three out-of-state businessmen were flying with me to Checats Lake on the mainland for a week's fishing outing when one of them leaned forward. "What are those orange balls down there?" he asked.

In a cove below floated half a dozen orange buoys marking the locations of crab pots. After I so informed the men, they conferred among themselves for a moment.

"Hey, could we stop and see if the pots have anything? Fresh crab for lunch at the lake would sure hit the spot." I explained that raiding the pots would constitute piracy. "Well," the men suggested, "we've got some liquor with us. Suppose we exchange a bottle of Scotch for some crab?"

That sounded like a fair arrangement to me, and I throttled back to land. Minutes later we took off again with three crab. Thereafter, the fisherman who operated the pots presumably kept his fingers crossed every time he pulled them up, just as bush pilots continued to report for work with curiousity piqued, wondering what would happen that day in the unpredictable world of bush flying.

OVERNIGHTING

· ·

Few pilots could find much humor in spending an unplanned night in the bush due to weather or mechanical problems. The aircraft were equipped with some emergency supplies, and most of us carried our own R-O-N (remain overnight) bags just in case, so survival was usually not a problem in the relatively mild environment of southeastern Alaska. Nonetheless, the experience left us grumbling. Because it was unexpected, we typically had to forgo activities we had planned in town — a movie date, a city league basketball practice, a woodworking project. Rarely did an overnighting occur at a place we would have chosen to visit on a day off. And the rotten weather that usually was responsible made spontaneous fun hard to find.

The mainland could be an especially lonely place to the pilot trying to sneak home through fog or snow with dusk around the corner. Run out of daylight in that wilderness and you usually had to spend the night by yourself. If you could, you reached a seasonal Forest Service or trapper's cabin. There you'd find enough provisions to make the experience a little less unpleasant: a small supply of wood for the stove, a candle or two, a few leftover cans of beans or soup, some magazines, maybe a fifty-one-piece deck of cards for a session of solitaire.

With no cabin at hand, home for the night was the least rock-ridden beach you could taxi to before darkness engulfed everything. Tie the airplane to a tree or rock, zip up your jacket, and curl up on the seats inside. Eat the spartan, hard, moldy emergency rations, if you wanted; you'd still listen to your stomach rumble. If the moon came out, you could also listen to the wolves howl.

In a fjord where a beach might not be available, the pilot could only drift about in the foggy dark, serenaded by unseen waterfalls.

The archipelago could also be lonely to the pilot who waited too long to concede defeat. He spent the night where he finally was forced to plop down, which could well be a boulder-ridden beach. He might have to stand shivering in the water throughout the night, holding the plane off the rocks as the tide came and went, cursing the rain and the wind and his job.

With human habitation rarely farther away than twenty or thirty miles, however, the islands offered plenty of options to the more prudent pilot who devoted the last few minutes of daylight or visibility to hightailing it to sanctuary. Virtually everyone maintained an open-door policy in the bush, where survival often depended on mutual help. At a camp or village a pilot would have shelter for the airplane, a warm bunk, and a hearty meal. In fact, bachelor pilots who had not evolved into competent cooks would likely eat more sumptuously while stuck overnight than they would have back in their apartments; bush tradition prohibited allowing a grounded pilot to leave the table until he had stuffed a third helping of everything down his throat.

The after-dinner agenda included conversation, competition at card games or Monopoly, perhaps a photo album of life back in Oregon to thumb through. For pilots so inclined, there might be a six-pack to share.

While the pilot snored away the evening, his hosts strolled down to the harbor to add another tiedown line to the airplane, sweep the snow off the wings and tail, and chase away kids who had sneaked into the cockpit to jiggle the controls.

Of course, some bush communities were more popular among pilots than others for overnight stays. Regardless of a pilot's religious conviction, Christian camps—those operated by believers who imposed strict rules of conduct—rated four stars for quality fellowship and accommodations. The few camps with alcoholic operators, on the other hand, could make you think of Dodge City with the marshal out of town. Sometimes in a burst of gusto a logger would whoop and fire a gun at the bunkhouse ceiling. You wondered how anyone there managed to make it to the woods in the morning.

The Haida Indian village of Hydaburg on Prince of Wales was one of the last civilized places at which my fellow pilots and I wanted to get stuck for the night. The village, twenty-two miles south of Craig, then had no hotel, restaurant, or entertainment, and the two general stores maintained irregular hours. Even more inhibiting than the absence of public amenities was the animosity some residents displayed toward Caucasians.

A few years earlier the village had launched a cultural-revival program to preserve its tribal traditions from the "Americanization" white teachers and missionaries had imposed with heavy-handedness in the early part of the century. According to residents, the whites had suppressed Haida dances, songs, legends, and other aspects of the culture. Elderly resident Helen Sanderson said the teachers "used to beat us for speaking Haida" when she was a schoolgirl in the village. A fuzzy document from the Haida archives, composed by whites and dated 1911 or 1915, read in part: "We . . . hereby declare that we have given up our old tribal relationships; that we recognize no chief or clan or tribal family, that we have given up all claim or interest in tribal and communal houses; that we live in one-family houses in accordance with the customs of civilization; that we observe the marriage laws of the United States; that our children take the name of the father and belong equally to the father and mother . . . that we have discarded the totem and recognize the Stars and Stripes as our only emblem . . ." The document contained the signatures of twenty-eight of the village's leading citizens.

Over the decades most Haida ancestral customs had thus faded into desuetude. Just a handful of the oldest villagers could still speak the Haida language, which, along with much community folklore, was written only in their waning memories or in the silent images of surviving Haida artifacts. One spring day Helen Sanderson and a friend approached Hydaburg school superintendent Dr. Leonard B. Waitman and asked if the school could teach Haida lore to children before it was lost forever. Waitman, who was white, thought the idea was not only feasible but overdue.

"It burned my ass," he said of the cultural-renunciation document.

With grants from the state (the Languages Department of the University of Alaska estimated the Haida language would be extinct in ten years unless it was recorded), the school inaugurated "Haida cultural study," in which pupils studied Haida cultural subjects one hour a day in class. Adults could participate through adult-education classes at night. The program's three instructors became the only certified Haida teachers in Alaska.

The village continued to live with modern conveniences and to pursue economic development with its share of the $1 billion and forty-four million acres of land the 1969 Alaska Native Claims Settlement Act had granted Alaska natives in exchange for land along the route of the trans-Alaska oil pipeline.

But the cultural revival generated a fierce community pride that resulted in a certain clannishness. A few of the 400 residents, perhaps those who were especially aware that Haidas once had a reputation among Indians as mighty warriors, developed resentment toward whites. The Ketchikan *Daily News* had published an article about tension between several residents and white teachers in the village.

In such an atmosphere, pilots preferred not to spend a night in Hydaburg and sought refuge elsewhere when bad weather caught them in the boondocks with dusk approaching. But mother nature honored no preferences.

One cool, overcast morning a Seattle-based inspector for the federal Occupational Safety and Health Administration chartered an airplane with the company to make routine safety checks at six communities on Prince of Wales. The Ketchikan Flight Service Station expected a gale to begin thrashing the region that evening, but the forecast for the day sounded okay. As the pilot I estimated we could complete the rounds and scoot back to town before the wind became unsafe.

I decided to start with the most distant destination on the itinerary and work our way toward Ketchikan so we would be drawing closer to home as the gale approached. That strategy left Hydaburg for last.

By the time we landed on Sukkwan Strait in front of the village around 5:45 P.M., raindrops were streaking off the windshield and whitecaps were foaming from the wave crests.

"Better hustle," I said to the inspector as I taxied the 185 toward the old seaplane dock in the harbor. "The gale's knocking on the door."

The inspector, a tall, middle-aged man whose suit seemed incongruous in the bush, hurried up the ramp while I paced about on the dock.

I was still pacing a half-hour later when the strait had become angry with waves and black gust streaks, and the hills toward Ketchikan had faded behind a curtain of gray stratus. Although an adjacent cold-storage building blocked the wind in the harbor, the trollers and seiners were rolling in their berths from the swells. The dock, too, was in constant motion, heaving as if King Neptune were trying to push it away; a couple of times the 185's wing—I was now staying beneath it for shelter from the rain—brushed my cap in a roll.

I glanced back at the village. A dog trotted across the driftwood-strewn beach, and in one of the ramshackle wooden houses bordering it, a woman stood by a window staring at me. But there was no sign of the inspector.

"Come on!" I muttered aloud.

When he finally stepped carefully down the ramp some thirty-five minutes later, holding up his briefcase as an umbrella, time had run out.

"Sorry I took so long," he said. "I had trouble finding the places I needed to inspect." He grimaced when I told him we would have to spend the night because of the weather and that Hydaburg had no public accommodations. "Do you know anyone we can stay with?"

The company's agent in the village was in the Lower Forty-eight, and the substitute agent was a sullen fellow who had become the brunt of jokes among our pilots. White teachers were on summer vacation. I knew about a dozen other residents who were frequent customers, but not the location of their homes. The prospect of knocking on doors at random to find out did not appeal to me.

"No, unfortunately. The people here are sort of unfriendly—they'll hardly give you the time of day. But I think I know a place where we can at least stay warm and dry."

The inspector said he had stopped at both general stores hoping to buy a snack and found them closed, so I reached into the baggage compartment, opened the emergency-survival kit, and took out the freeze-dried food. Next, I added a couple of lines to the three with which I had already tied the airplane, frowning at the dock's ceaseless undulating in the swells.

The inspector and I walked up the ramp, and I led the way down a path to a small building that housed long-distance telephone equipment for the village. From a previous charter with a telephone repairman, I knew where the door key lay cached, and we entered, dripping. Inside, a generator that supplied power to the equipment radiated welcome heat. I called the company on a phone there and explained our situation. Then we fashioned makeshift beds from overalls, a throw rug, and other pliable items, and heated water for the freeze-dried food in an electric coffee pot. Since the generator rendered conversation awkward, we idled away the hours reading magazines that were stacked on a table.

Later that night I trudged back to the dock to check the 185. Although it seemed secure enough in the rainy dark, I frowned again at that constant pitching and rolling. A few hundred feet away a loose strip of aluminum siding on the cold-storage building banged like rifle shots. What lousy luck to get weathered in *here*, I thought to myself. Anywhere else we would have had real beds, a hot meal, fellowship—and a decent berth for the airplane.

Back in the "Hydaburg Hilton," as we had dubbed the building, the humming from the generator eventually lulled me to sleep. When I awoke my watch read 6:15 A.M. A peek out the door revealed broken clouds and no wind, so I roused the inspector, and minutes later we headed back toward the dock.

At the tip of the ramp we stopped abruptly. The 185 was gone!

"What the hell!" I cried. I noticed immediately that half the dock was also missing. In dismay I quickly glanced about and spotted the airplane, apparently intact, about 200 yards away by the beach in front of the village, the heels of the floats pulled up on the gravel. Two men sat nearby on driftwood.

I jogged down the unpaved road that paralleled the beach, splashing through puddles, then cut across the pebbly sand until I reached the plane. The men stood up.

"You the pilot?" one asked. Both wore rain gear and had shoulder-length black hair.

"Yeah," I answered, panting. "What happened?"

Around midnight, they told me, the wind had reached sixty knots (the inspector and I hadn't heard it inside our noisy shelter) and a villager had gone down to the harbor to check the boats. He had seen that the dock was beginning to break up under the stress of the swells and, realizing the airplane was in jeopardy, had raced back to the village to get help. At least eight men had hurried into the stormy night, untied the plane, and using a skiff on either float, guided it to the beach. There, they had held it just offshore to prevent the waves from pounding the floats on the gravel. Several men had had to stand in the chilly water to grip the wing struts.

About 2 A.M. they had heard a loud crack, which they later discovered was a large section of the dock tearing away.

Finally, near dawn, the gale subsided, the water calmed, and the men had been able to beach the 185. The others had gone back to bed, but these two had remained behind to keep an eye on the plane and rebeach it every few minutes as the tide came in.

"Where were you?" one of the men asked. "We tried to find you last night but no one knew where you were staying."

"My passenger and I slept in that telephone shack south of the cold storage."

Both men looked puzzled. "Why did you sleep there?"

I shrugged my shoulders sheepishly. "Well, we didn't want to bother anyone."

The men were silent for a moment. "Anybody in the community would have put you up. We know you can't fly when it gets too windy." I thought I detected a hint of indignation in their faces.

"Did you think we'd scalp you?" the other man said with a slight smile.

I chuckled and thanked them with handshakes for their help, asking them to extend my thanks to the others. As they walked back toward the village, I signaled to the inspector, who still stood at the top of the ramp.

"I thought you said these people would hardly spare the time of day," he commented when I related the events of the night as we taxied out for takeoff.

On another inclement night long afterward, Hydaburg again showed love to someone who thought it absent. I had returned to Ketchikan the year before after a four-year absence. An unrelenting period of discontent with bush flying had prompted me to seek another career change, and a few weeks later New York City had become my new home. Four years on the staff of a major magazine-publishing organization based in Manhattan. Four years of jackets and ties and Scotches-on-the-rocks in trendy Upper East Side bars, where briefcase-toting yuppies crowded in at happy hour to unwind and socialize. Four years of smashing squash balls over lunch hours and banging at clay pigeons in Connecticut over weekends.

And four years of inner emptiness amid the bustle and tinsel. The emptiness had stayed on the shadowy side of my consciousness the first three years, occasionally nagging me like uncertain guilt while I struggled to catch up with my former classmates. But in the fourth year I finally admitted to myself that my heart wore a constant scowl in my new life. Ambling back to the office after a squash match and a stop at a deli for a take-out lunch, I would feel besieged by concrete and carbon monoxide and blaring horns. Entombed shoulder to shoulder in a lurching subway train with barely enough space to raise a hand to wipe the perspiration off my forehead, I would seethe with restrained rebellion. Standing in my boxy apartment on 87th Street looking out the window at uninterrupted columns of other boxy apartments, I would languish in spiritual claustrophobia.

Diversions like strolling in Central Park were limited by opportunity.

But I could escape anytime in daydreams about my beloved Alaska, so far away in distance and now in time. I remembered the invigorating smell of the archipelago air, and the chortle of a grizzled, whiskey-guzzling trapper as he described some misadventure, and the majesty of jagged, snowcapped peaks deep in the wilderness.

Sometimes reminiscing would wrench from me a forlorn sigh. But those days were gone, gone forever. I was closer to forty than thirty now. Already in middle age, by some standards, not far from crossing the line, according to others. Bush flying was a young man's game, reserved for romantics who were willing to put off real life for a few years. I had a good job and a career with a future now. How could I ever give them up? No, I could fly the bush again only in my photo albums, my logbooks, and my memories.

Yet other silent voices whispered that a job and career are "good" only if they're enjoyed. Pursuing a certain lifestyle simply for an image, the voices argued, is to be dishonest with oneself. People are individuals, with different interests, different abilities, and different roads to follow. If the absence of passion is a tragedy in life, then neglect of passion is a moral crime.

For months, returning to the cockpit in Alaska seemed as preposterous as returning to my college years. Grow up! I told myself. But wistful repetition gradually imbued the thought with possibility, and the inner emptiness began to fill with a growing dream. Inevitably, the north country sirens outsang the blaring horns and reached across the miles and years to pull me from the jostling crowds.

Like Flair Air, Revilla Flying Service in Ketchikan had just two airplanes, both 185s. One of them was berthed on a ramp in an aging waterfront hangar that also contained a loosely organized hodgepodge of airplane and engine parts, tools, fishing gear, construction supplies, welding equipment, paint cans, and outright junk, hanging on walls, standing in corners, piled on the bench, or stuffed into lockers. An office with desk, couch, filing cabinets, and coffee table was attached to the hangar. The second airplane sat on a ramp out back, between the hangar and Tongass Highway. A foot ramp led from the street down to the hangar and docks. Our facilities were sandwiched between those of my former company and another large air service.

Also like Flair Air, Revilla Flying Service had a limited crew to perform a variety of duties. I was the only pilot besides owner Dale D.

Clark, a thirty-three-year-old, bespectacled, curly-haired industrial-arts major from a Montana ranch family of twelve children. During the summer we employed a young Metlakatla woman to dispatch, answer the phone, and keep records. The rest of the year we did those things ourselves. When we were both out on flights, we turned on the telephone recorder and locked the office door.

A competent though unlicensed mechanic, Clark handled maintenance tasks during nonflying periods while I swept floors, shoveled snow, emptied garbage, and answered correspondence. I suffered no cultural shock from performing such menial chores. Alaska had wiped the scowl off my heart; now that I was back, wearing blue jeans literally and figuratively, I cherished even the rain.

Ketchikan had grown during my absence. Several new housing developments, their streets still unpaved, had eaten into the forested slopes, and a new shopping mall and a racquetball complex were in the offing. A fairly steady stream of cars poked along Tongass Avenue; people complained about the lack of parking spaces more than the weather. Much of the activity was in anticipation of an economic boom from U.S. Borax's planned mining of the world's largest known molybdenum deposit on the mainland forty miles to the east in Misty Fjords National Monument.

Business people regarded the mine as salvation, since the timber industry, one of Ketchikan's economic mainstays, had slumped. Only a few logging camps were still active on Prince of Wales, and dozens of unemployed loggers loitered in the unemployment office and the bars. I noticed that practically all of the remaining camps now had one or more TV satellite dishes.

Unchanged, as always, were the mountains, valleys, and forest, the islands, lakes, and waterways. I felt instantly at home among these familiar old friends. How strange to think I had ever left. Now it was New York that seemed a forbidding world away.

Since Revilla had no scheduled flights, we relied 100 percent on charters. They came in infinite variety, from short, local sightseeing tours to day-long trips into the upper panhandle. From spring to mid-fall, charters kept us in the air heading in all directions. On days when weather problems slowed us down, two, three, sometimes four backlogged groups of campers or fishermen waited in the hangar next to their piles of duffle bags, coolers, backpacks, cartons, beer cases, rifles, and fishing gear. Clark or I would taxi up to the dock, scramble out, and look at the crowd.

"Okay, who's next?"

I was content with a day off about every ten days.

Winter now. The lakes were frozen, the days dreary, the charters irregular. The week before Christmas brought a furious spurt of flying as people came in from the bush to catch jets or went out to the bush to spend the holidays at home. By Christmas Eve our thoughts focused on personal holiday activities. Clark made the only flight on the schedule, a 9 A.M. pickup at Metlakatla, then bid me merry Christmas. I lingered in the office for several hours in case the phone rang. In early afternoon I was finishing correspondence to prospective Lower Forty-eight customers when the door burst open. Out of breath, bundled up in a blue parka, lugging a suitcase and two shopping bags stuffed with brightly colored presents, a young native woman wore a desperate look.

"Can you fly me to Hydaburg?" she asked, her dark eyes fixed on my face.

I glanced at the clock on the wall and shook my head. "We're just about to shut down until the day after Christmas. I've got to do some shopping now. There are several other outfits in town. Why don't you try one of them?"

The woman's face contorted into a grimace. "They're already closed." She deposited her bags on the floor and stepped to the edge of the desk. Then she told me her name was Anna, that she hadn't been back to Hydaburg since high school five years before, that the holiday spirit in Seattle had made her homesick. Suddenly deciding to spend this Christmas in Alaska with her family, she had phoned the village yesterday and caught a 727 to Ketchikan this morning. Now she needed transportation the rest of the way, and Revilla was her last hope.

I looked at the clock again. If we left right now I could make the ninety-mile round trip with about a half-hour to spare before darkness. The stores would stay open late to accommodate last-minute shoppers like me. I teased Anna with a moment of hesitation before I smiled. "Okay, let's do it." A minute later Anna stood on the dock chatting excitedly while I loaded her suitcase and presents into the 185 and pumped twenty gallons of fuel into the left wing tank. She grinned like a child before a birthday party as we taxied into the Narrows for takeoff.

Once we were airborne, however, she grew strangely sullen. When I asked how it felt to be back in Alaska after five years, she simply shrugged. And, unlike most passengers, she showed little interest in the rocky beaches and snow-filled valleys around us. I assumed the noise of the engine discouraged her from talking and that she was preoccupied with thoughts of homecoming.

My own thoughts turned to the weather as we crossed Clarence Strait and approached Prince of Wales. The flurries that had been fluttering from the gray overcast all day were intensifying now, drawing a curtain across the island's hills and mountains. By the time we reached Hetta Inlet, visibility had dropped to a couple of miles. Unable to cut across the hills between Hetta and Sukkwan Strait directly to the village, I decided to follow the shoreline of the inlet all the way around.

But the snow continued to thicken, forcing us lower and lower until the floats practically touched the water. Trees, rocks, and driftwood along the shore slipped by like ghosts. The accumulation had already covered all exposed parts of the beach, right up to the water. I could see nothing out the windshield except thousands of thick flakes that seemed to be driving at us horizontally. Time to turn around.

I throttled back, lowered the flaps, and hugged the right shoreline in preparation for a left 180-degree turn. Then, suddenly, the ghosts vanished, leaving us enveloped in a whitish-gray vacuum. I yanked back the throttle and held up the nose. We plopped down firmly.

As I lowered the water rudders, Anna sat quietly, her hands in her lap, her eyes staring blankly at the instrument panel.

"It's getting pretty spooky out there, so we'll have to wait for the snow to let up a little," I said, turning the 185 toward the barely discernible shoreline. "The village is just around the corner, another fifteen miles or so, though I'm afraid we'll have to go back to town if things don't improve."

Anna raised her head to look out the windshield. When she spoke I had to cock my head to hear. "I want to go back to Ketchikan. I don't want to go to the village anymore. I've changed my mind. Please, take me back."

Shoulder-length black hair blocked her profile except for her nose. "Go back?" I said, bewildered. "Why? What happened? An hour ago you were begging me to fly you out."

"My family doesn't really want me. They said they do on the phone, just to be polite, but they don't. I'm the big-city girl now. I've become an outsider. I'd put a damper on their Christmas if I was there. I was a fool to think I could just waltz up here after so long and fit right back in."

"Aw, you're just nervous about greeting everyone," I said with a chuckle. "Once that's over, you'll think you never left."

Anna shook her head. "No. I don't belong anymore." Her voice was beginning to quiver. "I can see it all now. I guess I just had to get this close to realize it. Take me back, please." She turned to me and I noticed a glistening in her eyes.

But flying anywhere then was impossible. I paralleled the shore until I spotted a narrow, rock-free stretch where I could beach the floatplane.

Five times over the next two hours I crawled out on the wings to brush off a blanket of snow with my gloves so we would be ready to blast off as soon as the visibility improved. But the relentless snow collaborated with the fading light to turn our world into ever-deepening shades of gray. Soon dusk was upon us. Kicking driftwood at the edge of the forest, where I had been pacing, I cursed the weather. Now my passenger and I were stuck for Christmas Eve on a dark, cold beach in the boondocks. I thought of my friends and the lights and the holiday cheer back in town.

Anna merely nodded when, plastered with snow, I climbed into the cockpit and announced we would have to spend the night. My tidebook indicated that if I let the airplane go dry, the incoming tide would refloat it about dawn. The surrounding mountains and hills prevented direct communications with the Ketchikan Flight Service Station. But on the air traffic control center frequency for the area, I managed to contact an unseen airliner far above us. Crackling with static that seemed to punctuate our isolation, a voice with a southern accent agreed to let the Ketchikan FSS know of our predicament. Then we were alone again.

Neither of us had much of an appetite, but I pulled out some packets of snacks from the emergency supplies anyway, and Anna opened a present that contained a box of assorted chocolates. The hours dragged on and on. After the snow finally slackened, Anna and I spent part of the time stomping about in the night outside to stay warm. I assured her she could catch an Alaska Airlines flight back to Seattle the day after Christmas.

During one of our cockpit spells, each of us huddled in the dark with our thoughts, Anna suddenly began reminiscing about growing up in the village. She spoke of salmon fishing and berry picking and potlatch celebrations, of old people who could still converse in Haida and Christmas mornings in the family cabin overlooking Sukkwan Strait. I felt she was talking to herself as much as to me in her low, melancholy monotone.

I was dozing fitfully when Anna shook me.

"I hear a motor—listen."

In the otherwise quiet night a distant rumbling slowly grew louder. A boat was approaching. Wondering who could be out in this weather on Christmas Eve, I shined a penlight at my watch. It read 10:50. Moments later, lights appeared through the flurries. I recognized the outline of a salmon seiner. A spotlight sweeping the shoreline glared into the cockpit, and we shielded our eyes.

"There it is!" someone on the seiner called. "Hey, there!"

Anna and I clambered out and stood in the snow as a skiff putt-putted through the spotlight beam on the water up to the airplane. The bow crunched to a stop on the pebbles, and a middle-aged man wearing a rain suit and ski cap stepped onto the beach.

"Hi," he said to me. Then he looked at my passenger. "Anna!"

She hesitated. "It's my brother Frank!" They hugged for half a minute, then began talking softly. "How did you know where we were?" I heard her ask.

"We were waiting for you all day. When you didn't come we called Ketchikan, and the flight service station told us a Revilla plane was weathered in out here. We thought it was probably you trying to come home. You didn't think we'd let our little girl spend Christmas Eve out here in the snow, did you? Come on. Everybody at home is waiting for you."

I hauled Anna's suitcase and presents out of the rear seats and handed them to her brother, who took them to the skiff. Then I poked Anna in the ribs and whispered, "I thought you wanted to go back to town." She smiled and kissed me on the cheek.

"Do you need any help?" Frank asked me as he guided his sister into the skiff.

"Nope. I'll be okay. Merry Christmas."

When I awoke in the cockpit, shivering and famished, the sky was clear and a magnificent fluffy white coat adorned the beach, the trees, the hills. In every direction I gazed on a panoramic painting that sparkled in the early-morning sunlight. I grinned at the scene.

I was still grinning in my heart on the flight back to Ketchikan as I savored the richness of an interesting occupation. I knew that Anna, surrounded by love in her home on Christmas Day, also felt rich.

BAREFOOT HERO

That guy must be crazy!" the passenger said. We were sitting in a cafe in Craig, sipping coffee, waiting for a September squall to pass. The archeologist had chartered us to fly to the fishing village to assess several Tlingit artifacts a resident had found, and she had asked me to wait for her. When she returned to the cafe where we had arranged to meet, gusts were exceeding forty knots. We had ordered coffee and positioned ourselves at a window table to watch the weather.

"Who's crazy?" I asked.

The archeologist, a thin, thirtyish woman with wire-frame glasses, pointed out the window. "Him. That pilot. He looks like he's going to land here."

In the driving rain by the north end of Fish Egg Island, a floatplane was on final approach for the Craig waterfront. As we watched, the aircraft twisted and lurched in the wind as if doing aerobatics. The wings flipped sharply to a near-vertical position in one gust. Below the plane, the inlet churned from shoreline to shoreline in angry, foaming, two-foot waves.

"Can he land safely out there?" the archeologist asked.

I shook my head. "Even the seagulls are on the ground right now."

The plane descended to about ten feet above the water. Closer and closer it came, turning this way and that. Land, I silently urged, before you fly into the dock. At the last second it plopped down in a tiny bight by the seaplane dock, the only spot where the water was sheltered. I recognized the orange-and-white colors of Todd's Air Service's 185.

"Oh, that's Ed Todd," I said. "Wouldn't you know."

The plane maneuvered to the dock, and out jumped a man in short pants and bare feet.

"Now I *know* he's crazy!" the archeologist said. After tying up the 185, the pilot helped two passengers step from the cabin. They shook his hand and hurried up the ramp, hunching against the wind and rain.

I laughed. "That's Todd, all right, but he's not crazy."

Eccentric and colorful, Edwin Victor Todd knew exactly what he was doing. When bad weather kept other pilots huddled inside, he took off with calculated assurance. When a hunter or prospector wanted transportation to a lake the rest of us deemed too small to work safely, we referred him to Todd. A legend throughout Alaska, he had the experience and skills to do flying jobs the rest of us couldn't, and the sangfroid for those we wouldn't.

"We fly when YOU want to fly," read the Yellow Pages ad for Todd's Air Service. No matter that the wind was gusting to forty knots, or that dense rainfog forced motorists in town to use headlights at noon, or that the sun had already set behind the western mountains. In marginal situations, when we stood by the window in the office, weighing the risks against the potential rewards, the sight of anyone else's floatplane taxiing out into the Narrows often goaded us into launching one of our own planes for a look; weather that was good enough for a neighboring air service was good enough for us. Todd exerted no such influence when *he* flew by, however. He had different standards and belonged to a different class, an image psychologically supported by the location of his operation south of town some three miles from where the other Ketchikan air taxis were clustered along the waterfront.

Sometimes a group of weather-grounded pilots would gather in a waterfront restaurant and watch Todd's 185 disappear up the channel in the fog. Then we'd speculate on how he was able to get through in conditions that blocked the rest of us like a concrete wall.

"He's got super eyesight, that's all," someone would proclaim. "Nah," another pilot said, "I think he's got a photographic memory; he doesn't need to see where he's going, except for a rock here and a tree there."

118

A third pilot suggested he flew much of the time on instruments, and someone else claimed the man "just plain has more balls than we do."

Not always did Todd get away with it. While he never scratched a passenger in his twenty-five-year career, he sometimes returned with a damaged airplane. Taking off one day from a small lake with an overload of deer carcasses, he underestimated the room he needed. The floats struck rocks on the shore just as the airplane left the water. Quick reflexes and a superb flying ability enabled him to stay aloft and struggle back to town. Although the floats were torn, he ramped the plane before it could sink.

Undoubtedly there were incidents we never heard about, but none seemed to temper Todd's ways.

As if to flaunt his defiance of the elements, Todd typically flew in short pants and bare feet, although in especially nasty, cold weather he donned overalls and a pair of sandals. Throughout the year he took daily skinny dips in the frigid waters of Tongass Narrows, and he jumped rope regularly. He eschewed tobacco, coffee, and junk food. Wiry and tough, beady-eyed and crafty-looking, sporting an Errol Flynn mustache, Todd was ruggedly handsome despite a short, slightly round-shouldered frame. He spoke with a western accent and called most males "partner."

Like most owners of small air services, he worked tirelessly fourteen to sixteen hours a day, week after week during the Season. He attracted lots of business, invested wisely, and left a valuable estate. But it was joie de vivre rather than wealth that drove him.

"Because it's interesting," he told me one day during a recorded interview when, as a reporter, I asked him why he had put up with the long hours, stormy weather, and insecurity for so many years. "You get a charter into some place where you seldom go and sometimes where you never have been before . . . I think about selling out, and then I think, my god, what would I do that was more interesting . . . . If I get a good offer I might do it and go into the real estate business, but shoot, I don't think I'd enjoy myself in it like I am here. People have asked me, 'Todd, why don't you retire?' and I say, 'For god's sake, what's retirement but sitting here in an airplane and watching the scenery rolling by?'

"I had a guy come up here one time and he stayed with me about a week, a guy I hadn't seen in years. When he left he cranked hands with me and he said, 'I don't know anybody that lives a better life than you do,' and that just about put it in the words that I felt about it."

Todd liked to fly low to see more details, and even in sunny weather he often hugged a shoreline for miles to look at the driftwood and rocky niches. He was not averse to buzzing a bear or a friend's house; oldtimers still chuckle about the time a young Todd buzzed a girlfriend's home in the Herring Cove section of Ketchikan and ran into telephone wires he had failed to notice. He recovered quickly enough to avoid crashing.

While other pilots took a break from airplanes on their days off, Todd would jump into a 185 on his (when he allowed himself a day off) and explore someplace he had never been. Ken Loken, president of Channel Flying in Juneau, once landed in Twin Glacier Lake near the Taku River with a load of passengers and found Todd and a female companion skinny dipping off a 185.

Todd's spirit soared no less outside the cockpit. He drove two Datsun "Z" sports cars, one purple, one white ("my roller skates, one for one foot and one for the other"). He took winter vacations in Tahiti, Spain, and other exotic places, often pausing to visit a nudist colony on the way. And he seized every opportunity for practical jokes. Snorkling one day near his flying service, he spotted someone beachcombing. It was dowager Katherine Ziegler, widow of a pioneer Ketchikan attorney. Todd swam over to her underwater, jumped up by the shore, and growled like a monster.

Although he rarely socialized at other air taxis, Todd liked people. Several pilots in Ketchikan and on the airlines might have had to enter other professions if he had not helped them learn to fly. He had sold me my Luscombe for much less than it was worth.

Todd's Air Service maintained an open-door policy, and on a typical night a handful of friends, fellow pilots, and customers gathered in the kitchen of the house above the hangar to sip tea or munch a salmon filet or mountain goat steak. Todd would describe a tough flight he had made that day, his face affecting a grimace for emphasis but his eyes twinkling. Then there would be a rap on the door. Todd would get up, and a moment later we would hear, "Hey, partner, come on in!" One night he put on a huge sombrero he had brought back from Mexico and pranced around the room mimicking an ape while we howled with laughter.

A poetry lover, he often recited verse during such theatrics. He was especially fond of Robert Service's "The Men That Don't Fit In." Ask Todd if he was ever going to retire from bush flying to live a "normal" life, and he'd open his mouth in mock astonishment, point a questioning finger at his chest, and rant histrionically:

There's a race of men that don't fit in,
A race that can't stay still,
So they break the heart of kith and kin,
And they roam the world at will.
They range the field and they rove the flood,
And they climb the mountain's crest;
Theirs is the curse of the gypsy blood,
And they don't know how to rest.

Born in Seattle on May 2, 1919, Todd moved to Ketchikan with his family as a boy. After working at various construction jobs, he learned to fly and established his air service. He also attracted a mate who shared his love of adventure. Helen Todd, however, lacked her husband's skill. Or maybe his luck. One afternoon she left in a Piper Super Cub for nearby Annette Island to check her trapline. When she hadn't returned by evening, Todd took off to search for her, but dusk and fog had already blackened the island. In the morning he found her lifeless body on a lake beach, her Super Cub upside down in the water. Apparently she had lost her depth perception on approach to the lake (which afterward gained the name "Helen Todd Lake") and flown into the glassy water, flipping the airplane. Without matches or dry clothing, she died of exposure during the night.

It was then, some friends claimed, that Todd began his regimen of exposing his flesh to the elements to toughen it lest it someday be called upon to suffer the same trial. Other friends said Todd flew in short pants and bare feet simply because he was sensually oriented.

Two years after the tragedy, another woman entered his life. Dixie Jewett, a native of Virginia City, Montana, had left her job as an artist in the ad section of a large department store in the Southwest and headed for Anchorage to escape the heat and boredom. Her money took her only as far as Ketchikan, so she worked there as a cab driver and sign painter.

One day Todd needed a business sign painted, and he called her. Enchanted by the tall, pixie-eyed, bushy-haired woman, he invited her along on a flight. Then he offered her a job as dispatcher. She, in turn, fell in love with the daring, lusty pilot, who at forty-eight was twice her age. Eager to impress him, she decided to learn to fly and took informal lessons from his assistant pilot, Tony Kielczewski.

Soon she was spending more time practicing takeoffs and landings than dispatching. Realizing she was hooked, Todd bought an $1800 Piper

Super Cruiser in Pennsylvania through a classified ad in a national aviation marketing newspaper.

"Go pick it up and don't come back without your license," he told her.

By nature as plucky as Todd himself, Jewett accepted the challenge. Despite her inexperience, she returned to Ketchikan from the 4000-mile flight with a commercial license and the airplane and her body intact. But one January day Kielczewski did not come back. About 10:30 A.M. he loaded a 185 with groceries and took off in gusty, bitterly cold weather for Hyder and the abandoned salmon cannery at Hidden Inlet on Portland Canal, where a family still lived. A message he left on the telephone recorder in the office stated he planned to return around 3 P.M. He never reached either destination.

Vacationing in California when they heard the news, Todd and Jewett hurried back to join the search. For days search aircraft battled turbulent north winds, snow squalls, and early darkness. But no one spotted a trace of the plane in the vast wilderness of icy mountains and thickly forested valleys between Ketchikan and Portland Canal. Vessels scouring Portland Canal and Revillagigedo Channel found no wreckage in the water. After several weeks the search was cancelled.

With Kielczewski gone, Todd's Air Service needed another assistant pilot, and Jewett took over. Bush flying was a man's domain. Jewett was the first female pilot in Ketchikan since aviation had begun in the community almost half a century earlier, and initially many customers declined to ride with her. But she flew to the same destinations in the same weather as the men and showed both spunk and ability.

"It was no time at all before these people were asking for her," Todd reminisced later. "They'd say, 'I don't want you, you SOB, send that good-looking pilot over here,' and that's the way it's been ever since. Nobody ever refused to ride with her again. In fact, a lot more people request her than ever requested me."

Jewett added that once she gained acceptance, "about two hundred people claimed to have been the first to fly with me."

Over the years, Todd's Air Service gained fame and a certain notoriety as Ketchikan's most colorful flying duo: the hearty, barefoot Todd, who flew when even the seagulls tucked their wings; and the spunky Jewett, who proved to tough, skeptical loggers and fishermen that she could fly as well as a man. Like the rest of us hired hands, Jewett sometimes became disgruntled with bush flying. Several times she quit in a huff, vowing to forsake "this thankless job," as she called it. But always, after a few weeks in another livelihood in another town, she was back, lured not only by the sirens but by her love for Todd.

To her, and to everyone else, Todd was an indestructible hero, as indelibly a part of Ketchikan as Deer Mountain and Tongass Narrows. Thus, when he failed to return from a routine flight one mid-October Sunday, hours passed before she became concerned. Todd had taken off alone about 7:30 A.M. to hunt mountain goats and planned to pick up two sport fishermen at Fish Creek in Thorne Arm at noon on the way back.

For a while Jewett assumed Todd had simply spent too much time stalking a big billy and had fallen behind schedule. When there was still no trace of his 185 by late afternoon, however, she concluded he was grounded somewhere by a broken fuel injector, ignition trouble, or other mechanical problem. It had happened to Todd before; it had happened to her.

She took off in the air service's other 185 and landed at Fish Creek. No, the fishermen said, they had not seen Todd's orange-and-white airplane. After dropping the fishermen back in town, Jewett called two fellow pilots, and that evening the three airplanes searched Todd's favorite mountain-goat lakes in the Coast Mountains. Todd had not specified a lake from which he would hunt because, like most hunters, he flew from lake to lake until he found the quarry within stalking distance. After dark Jewett reluctantly notified the Ketchikan Volunteer Rescue Squad that Todd was overdue.

Had any other pilot been missing, the news would have dismayed the shell-shocked residents of Ketchikan and stung their wounds. Already that year, the town had suffered four fatal air crashes, three of which occurred during a single terrible week in August. In the worst accident, a Grumman Goose slammed into fog-bound Sumner Strait, killing all twelve occupants. The other crashes claimed thirteen additional lives.

But nobody was worried about the fifty-nine-year-old Ed Todd, who looked forty-five and acted thirty; he was the best bush pilot of them all, a veteran of thirty years and 30,000 hours of tough, stormy flying. He was okay. Besides, people reminded themselves, Sunday's weather had been excellent. The first fourteen days of the month dumped more than eleven inches of rain on the area, but not a drop fell on the fifteenth, although scattered fog clung in some of the valleys. If Todd could work mountain lakes with heavy loads in nasty conditions, he certainly could handle mountain lakes alone in good weather.

The skies remained calm and dry when the official search finally got under way shortly after noon on Monday, more than twenty-four hours after Todd missed his Fish Creek pickup. Normally, the Ketchikan Volunteer Rescue Squad would have launched a search at dawn, but members shared the initial assumption that Todd had encountered some mechanical problem. So, they waited while Jewett searched again that morning. When she once more reported no sign of her boss or his 185, N70269, the KVRS went into action.

Organized in 1947 following the crash of a Pan American World Airways DC-4 on Annette Island, the privately funded KVRS included air taxi pilots, state troopers, city firemen, and other citizens able to help out in rescue operations. Over the years the KVRS had located scores of hunters, fishermen, boaters, hikers, and pilots missing in the wilderness surrounding Ketchikan, a wilderness too vast for the Coast Guard alone to cover.

The area the KVRS now had to scour extended from Ketchikan north to Bradfield Canal, east to Portland Canal, and south to Filmore Inlet: some 7000 square miles of mountains, forest, and waterways. Much of the area lay within the Misty Fjords National Monument, and the geography gave the older searchers a sense of déjà vu; it was here they had looked unsuccessfully for Tony Kielczewski almost ten years earlier.

Throughout Monday afternoon twenty-five airplanes and helicopters scouted dozens of lakes, both named and unnamed. Each aircraft carried a spotter so that in the passes and valleys and bowls, with cliffs and peaks all around, the pilot could concentrate on flying. Searchers also investigated a sighting of flashing lights on Annette Island and a report by campers at Humpback Lake of two rifle shots to the east.

No one found Ed Todd.

At seven-thirty that evening the pilots and spotters crowded into search headquarters in the dispatching office of Temsco Helicopters on Peninsula Point north of town. White-haired, droopy-eyed, hawk-nosed Dick Borch leaned on the office side of the counter while the others stood or sat on the lounge side. A long-time ferry and tugboat skipper, Borch helped organize the KVRS in 1947 and had served as its leader ever since.

"Let's see what we have," he said in his characteristic slow rasp. "Todd took off shortly after dawn. The people that live near his hangar heard him depart. What we don't know is where he went. The note he left only said he was going goat hunting and would be back at noon to pick up a couple of guys at Fish Creek. As far as Dixie can tell, he didn't have any passengers. Nobody heard any radio transmissions from him, and we haven't received any reports of an ELT [emergency locator transmitter, a required piece of equipment on most U.S. civil aircraft. On impact it automatically emits a continuous signal on the international mayday frequency]. We asked the airlines to listen for signals when they're over this area, but they monitor the emergency frequency anyway."

Borch studied the large chart spread out on the counter. The portion that depicted the search area contained a grid pattern in blue pencil, each quadrant representing the responsibility of one search aircraft.

"If he had to be back at noon he probably didn't go too far—somewhere within fifty miles. The weather was pretty good, so that wasn't a factor. But Dixie checked all the lakes he likes to hunt from yesterday and this morning, and we checked them again this afternoon. We also checked more distant lakes. So far we have no clues. Anybody got any ideas?"

One pilot suggested Todd had landed on a river rather than a lake, but Borch dismissed that possibility because snowfall had not yet forced goats to an elevation low enough to justify stalking from a river. Another searcher wondered if Todd had been unable to locate goats within stalking range and decided to visit friends at a camp or settlement instead.

"We've already contacted the few people who live within reasonable flying distance of the mainland," Borch said. "None of them saw Todd or heard an airplane Sunday."

Had Todd encountered engine trouble somewhere between Ketchikan and the mainland and been forced down on salt water or muskeg? Maybe. From now on searchers would start looking for N70269 as soon as they took off, not just upon reaching mountain goat country.

Then one pilot reported that late-afternoon fog had prevented him from inspecting a small lake in his section. Borch asked him to point out the lake, and as the other searchers crowded around the chart, the pilot tapped a location in the Boca de Quadra area about seven miles east of Humpback Lake.

"Well, that could mean something," Borch said. "The shots those guys at Humpback heard may have come from there, though that's pretty far for a rifle report to carry. Okay, let's have a real good look at that one first thing in the morning, if we can; the weather forecast doesn't sound too promising."

Most searchers might as well have stayed in bed Tuesday morning. The hills and mountains had disappeared behind ragged stratus that raced above the treetops at 400 to 700 feet, and heavy rain, driven horizontally by southeasterly gusts of thirty knots, cut visibility to a mile or less. The KVRS dispatched just seven aircraft, and the pilots, the organization's most experienced, had to stick to the shorelines.

Meanwhile, about 11:30 A.M. Tuesday, a salmon troller sighted what appeared to be an oil slick off the mouth of Ella Creek on Revillagigedo Island and radioed the news to Ketchikan. Two hours later, a ground party dropped off by helicopter investigated the discoloration; it originated from a recent mudslide 300 yards upstream.

As the seven aircraft crews returned one by one to refuel, other KVRS members handed them sandwiches the Hilltop Motel and the Seventh-Day Adventist Church had donated.

In midafternoon KVRS vice-president Ken Eichner, president of Temsco Helicopters and a three-decade veteran of flying in the Ketchikan area, finally managed to work his Hughes 500C chopper up the valleys and sneak through a pass to the lake east of Humpback. There, he slowly turned 360 degrees, watching the shoreline as it swung across the windshield. He spotted an old slide, a beaver dam, and two geese, which swam nervously away from the strange, noisy bird.

But he saw no airplane.

Less than fifteen miles to the north, the wreckage of a twin-engine Lockheed Electra lay on a mountainside above Badger Bay, a crumpled, rusting reminder of an earlier search for another famous pilot. On a stormy January 5, 1943, Harold Gillam, one of Alaska's premier pioneer bush pilots, crashed there during a flight from Seattle to Anchorage. He survived the crash, but it took searchers more than a month to find him. By then he had frozen to death.

By now news of the search for Todd had spread throughout Southeast and reached dozens of people in the rest of Alaska and the Pacific Northwest. Again and again a ringing telephone interrupted the Ketchikan *Daily News* reporter covering the story. Friends, former passengers, admirers, and relatives asked if Todd had been found and, learning that he had not, lingered on the line to pay tribute:

"Hell, nothing can hurt ol' Todd. I used to fly with him when I was setting chokers out at Cape Pole. He come out and got me and Jake Rauwolf one day when it was blowing and snowing like mad. No one else would turn a prop, but we called Todd and he come right out and got us in his 185. Yeah, Todd's okay, wherever he is."

Eventually the reporter told the front office to screen her calls and refer to the newsroom only those that related to search developments. The phones also rang repeatedly at KVRS headquarters at Temsco Helicopters; residents offered their services as spotters, sandwich-makers, or in whatever other capacity help might be needed.

Tuesday night the searchers again gathered in Temsco's dispatching office, tracking in mud and dripping rainwater on the floor. In a few minutes the windows fogged over. Borch paced about on the office side of the counter as he spoke.

"I'm afraid the weather doesn't look any better for tomorrow, just more of the same garbage. It looks like we'll have to run the beaches again, but we're getting to the point now where that might turn up something. If Todd's up there in one of those little mountain lakes, he knows it might be a week or more before the weather lets us get to him, so he just might try to walk out. But the way he dresses, he's going to have a rough time. There's fresh snow up there. Dixie, he doesn't carry much survival gear, does he?"

"Flippers, that's it. He's a poor swimmer. He doesn't like any extra weight when he comes out of the potholes he goes into. But he's a toughie. He could last a lot longer than most pilots in their twenties all bundled up."

When Jewett returned to Todd's Air Service after the meeting, about thirty friends and relatives were chatting quietly and sipping coffee in small groups, as various people had been doing all day there. Todd's half-brother, Leon Snodderly, a first officer for Alaska Airlines, had arrived from Seattle on Monday, but the other relatives had gotten in only that morning. Several women were making fresh coffee in the kitchen or offering cold cuts and cheeses on trays in the living room. Around midnight the last visitor left. The doorbell began ringing again about 9 A.M.

Elsewhere Tuesday night, the Los Angeles Dodgers were playing the New York Yankees in the sixth and, as it turned out, final game of the World Series. Television sets in Ketchikan bars were on to catch the satellite broadcast, but the game was anticlimactic; patrons and bartenders talked instead about a bush pilot missing somewhere in the mountains.

Dawn overslept Wednesday morning. When the lingering night finally withdrew, allowing searchers to see out the windows of Temsco's dispatching office, Tongass Narrows resembled the open North Pacific. Deep, rolling swells rushed by, foam spraying from the crests in a steady thirty-knot wind, and Gravina Island, a half-mile away on the opposite shore, was invisible behind the murky rainfog.

The weather did not keep the Coast Guard base in Ketchikan from sending out a cutter to search the maze of shorelines along the mainland, but it delayed until 11:30 A.M. the arrival of two huge HH3F helicopters from the Coast Guard air station at Sitka. Only the KVRS's four most experienced pilots took off, and for the second day in a row their searching was limited to the shorelines.

The four KVRS planes worked in two pairs, with one aircraft in each team following the other. The theory was this: If Todd had hiked down from the mountains and was huddled in the forest, he might not be able to scamper through the windfall to the beach before the first plane passed. But he probably would get there in time to wave his arms at the second one, following a mile behind. For safety in the poor visibility, the lead aircraft and the trailing one tried to stay at different altitudes—not an easy task when you could climb no higher than treetop level anyway.

The pilots in each team stayed in contact with one another by radio. In some areas mountaintop radio repeater facilities relayed the transmissions to Ketchikan. Leaning back in his chair with his hands clasped behind his head, Borch listened by the radio at Temsco:

"Six-Six Xray, Eight-Two Fox, I've lost sight of you, Mike, what's your position?"

"We're coming up on Smeaton Bay."

"Say again?"

"Smeaton Bay, Smeaton Bay."

"Roger, understand Smeaton. We're just about there, too. Be advised we're down to 200 feet now. We'll try to slow down and let you get a little more ahead of us."

Borch, who had not lost a search aircraft in the entire history of the KVRS, recalled the four planes about 3:30 P.M. The Coast Guard helicopters, also forced to stick to the shorelines, came back in not long afterward.

No strategy meeting took place that night because the forecast called for continued rain, fog, and wind on Thursday, which again would limit searching to the beaches. Although Todd had now been missing for four days, most people in Ketchikan remained confident he would be located alive and well. He would be on a beach or at the edge of a mountain lake or in a muskeg meadow, lightly dressed, a cocky grin on his face. "Well, partner, it took you guys long enough to find me," he'd say with a twinkle in his eye to the pilot who picked him up.

Borch told representatives of the news media the KVRS felt discouraged with the weather but not with the prospect of finding Todd alive.

"Todd's one of the most experienced, capable pilots in Alaska," he said. "All we need is good weather."

Borch got it Thursday. Contradicting the gloomy forecast, the morning brought mere broken clouds and isolated showers, with excellent ceilings and visibility. The KVRS quickly dispatched seventeen aircraft, the Coast Guard choppers took off from the Ketchikan airport, and the cutter sped out of the harbor at Base Ketchikan.

Don Ross, part owner of Ketchikan Air Service and next to Todd the most seasoned pilot in the Ketchikan area, preferred to fly alone, without a spotter. On Monday, the last time the weather gods had smiled on Ketchikan, he had searched the lakes in his quadrant looking for a beached 185. Now he checked those lakes again in his own 185, paying more attention to the rocky slopes around the lakes. About 10:15 A.M. he circled a small, unnamed lake at the 3000-foot level several miles north of Big Goat Lake. Sighting nothing there, he flew out the V-shaped mouth of the lake and began studying the valley slopes below.

"A couple of miles down the valley I saw a different color on the rocks, something that didn't belong," Ross said. "I came back for a closer look and saw an orange wingtip. After another pass I saw pieces of metal scattered all over the mountain."

"Roger," Borch said quietly at Temsco when Ross radioed the discovery. After a moment of silence, the KVRS chief cancelled the search, directing Ross, Eichner, and two additional pilots to proceed to Big Goat Lake for the recovery effort.

Jewett, searching in the same quadrant because it contained Todd's favorite goat lakes, was flying with Cape Pole resident Larry Simpson as a spotter. They failed to hear the transmission because of terrain interference. A few minutes after Ross sighted the wreckage, she circled the same unnamed lake and then flew down the valley. Jewett admired Simpson's cool nerve as a spotter. He kept his eyes constantly glued to the windows, unperturbed by bumps, steep banks, or sudden applications of power. Spotters who turned away for a couple of seconds to see what the airplane was doing might miss something important. Now Simpson spoke as he spotted the bits of metal.

"I see wreckage."

Shocked, dismayed, Jewett circled several times and reported the sighting to Temsco. It was then she learned Ross had already found N70269.

Most of the KVRS fleet had heard Ross's transmission; when Eichner lowered his Hughes 500C helicopter onto a rocky peninsula at Big Goat Lake, five or six floatplanes were beached in a line on the nearby southern shore, two others were taxiing in, and two more were circling to land. A dozen pilots and spotters stood in a group by the airplanes. Three searchers climbed into the 500C, and Eichner took off for the crash site.

The wreckage lay vertically strewn on the steep slope from an elevation of about 3700 feet—almost within throwing distance of the ridge's crest—down to about 2500 feet. Eichner could land no closer than a half-mile from the scene; the party needed four hours to struggle up to what used to be a Cessna 185 floatplane.

After cutting the seatbelt and extracting Todd's overalls-clad body from the cockpit, the crew, in one member's words, "kicked the airplane down the mountain" so that the dislodging effects of the prying and wrenching they had done would not cause the wreck to tumble suddenly onto them as they descended. As one searcher slung the body over his shoulder, a large jackknife fell out of the overalls and clattered onto the rocks. Goat's hair and dried blood covered the blade.

No one could explain the crash. Jewett, noting that N70269 was the lesser performer of Todd's Air Service's two 185s, suggested the floats struck the rocks at the edge of the tiny unnamed lake on takeoff and Todd tried to keep the plane in the air.

"He just never throttled back," she said. "Once, coming out of a lake, he even ran up on the muskeg, but he kept barreling along till he got her in the air. He always just kept boring ahead."

Other pilots speculated fog had formed in the valley and that Todd, trying to climb through on instruments, as he had on hundreds of other occasions in various situations, had finally met the law of averages. An autopsy determined no medical problems that might have contributed to the accident.

Officials from the National Transportation Safety Board and FAA arrived in Ketchikan on Friday to investigate, but the resulting NTSB report listed the cause of the accident as undetermined.

To people throughout Alaska, the puzzle was not why it had happened, but that it had happened at all. Pilots felt especially humbled. Some of us had regarded Todd as a larger-than-life figure, an heroic knight invincible before all dragons and ogres. If *he* could fall on a seemingly innocuous mission, no amount of savvy could ever protect the rest of us from the menaces of the bush.

Ketchikan's Chapel of the Mortuary overflowed during services the following week. Dozens of mourners unable to squeeze in stood outside in a light rain on the steps and sidewalks. The pastor read a eulogy I had written. Afterward, Todd's ashes were deposited in his wife's grave in Bayview Cemetery south of town.

Ketchikan writer Margaret Bell Wiks, author of twelve books, also wrote a eulogy:

> Ed Todd is dead.
> The whole town's crying.
> Icarus, soaring toward the sun,
> Falling, dying.

> Ed Todd is gone.
> The whole town's crying.
> Angels go along to guard his way,
> Flying, flying.

Jewett, who inherited a portion of Todd's estate, left Ketchikan and commercial flying for good to pursue an art career. She lived for several years in Bozeman, Montana. When the Big Sky hills and sage became too familiar, she wandered about other parts of the West.

Meanwhile, former Ketchikan pilot Joe Soloy had started a company in Washington State to provide turbine-engine conversions for piston-powered helicopters. When Soloy Conversions expanded into airplane turbine conversions, the company's first demonstrator was a Cessna 185. Soloy named it the *Ed Todd* for his old friend.

"If Ed had had this airplane with all its extra power, who knows, he might be alive today," Soloy said.

Yet at fifty-nine, Todd would have had only a few years' flying left. Soon he would have been eligible for social security, a thought incongruous with his exuberant lifestyle. At least he had died quickly, in an airplane, while still healthy in body and mind, doing what he loved in a place he loved. Death was not always so kind.

MECHANICALS

n the early days of aviation, some pilots carried a mechanic on every flight. With just cause, they worried more about the health of their rickety, wood-and-fabric airframes and unreliable engines than they did about the weather. Modern, all-metal, scientifically engineered airplanes, however, flew on and on and on with little protest. They tolerated the pounding of waves and swells, and the engines withstood the intense heat of long, low-speed, high-power climbs and the shock-cooling of long, high-speed, low-power descents.

On modern airplanes used in air taxi work, engines were legally limited to a finite number of hours before they had to be overhauled or rebuilt, regardless of condition: 1700 for the Cessna 185s and 206s IO-520 Continental, and 1500 for the de Havilland Beaver's Pratt & Whitney R-985. Airframes had to be inspected every 100 hours of flight time. Some modern bush planes still on the line had accumulated more than 15,000 hours, and some pilots with that many hours had never experienced a major in-flight mechanical problem. Yet, we could not help mentally squirming while flying over an angry ocean, a thick forest, or a rugged mountain.

Labouchere Bay was a large, open body of water at the north end of Prince of Wales, interrupted only by a few islets. Protected from the swells of Sumner Strait, to which it opened, and from the prevailing southeast wind except in a gale, the bay offered a floatplane pilot plenty of room in which to take off, with ample space left over for a safety margin. At the head of the bay sat a logging camp.

It was here that I had taken two Coast Guard officers on the second stop of a charter to inspect fuel storage facilities. We had landed first in Bay of Pillars at Kuiu Island at an abandoned salmon cannery, where some storage tanks still contained fuel. While the officers poked around the tanks in their blue uniforms and orange jackets, checking for leaks and undermining of the structures, I had browsed through dew-laden bushes plucking blueberries and salmonberries. The partly cloudy skies were dry, my thoughts far from mechanical problems. At Labouchere Bay an hour later I had passed the standby time by jogging on the camp's logging roads.

Now, the second inspection completed, my hair still wet from a shower in a bunkhouse, we taxied from the dock. Next was the tiny hamlet of Point Baker, just three miles to the north. The 185's engine responded normally with full power as I pushed the throttle to the firewall, and moments later the floats slipped off the water. At that point I automatically took my right hand off the throttle to retract the flaps.

Suddenly, the snarl of the engine dropped to a sputter. Thinking a loose friction lock on the throttle assembly had allowed the plunger to slip back to the idle position, I shot my hand from the flap lever back to the throttle. It found the throttle, as well as the prop and mixture controls, still firewalled. We had climbed only a few feet above the water, and before I could take other action the airplane dropped back down on it. The idling engine sputtered again as if choking, then stopped.

The incident had lasted a few seconds, barely enough time for an instant of terror had we been over rocks or trees or ocean swells. But noting the large body of gentle water all around I had felt no tension on takeoff, and no adrenaline flowed when the power loss occurred. Instead, there was only surprise, which kept us silent for several moments while the gyros whined down inside the instrument panel.

"What happened?" one of the officers finally asked. Each of the fuel gauges indicated a half-full tank, and the handle on the fuel-selector mechanism still pointed at "both," meaning the engine had drawn fuel from both tanks simultaneously. The emergency fuel-shutoff valve remained in the "off" position.

"I'm not sure, but we'll find out," I answered. Aware that the Coast Guard was a frequent and valuable customer for Revilla Flying Service, I added with a chuckle, "This has never happened to me before." The engine, an overhauled Continental IO-520-D installed a few days earlier to replace it run-out predecessor, had accumulated about ten hours—all trouble-free. I was leery of trying to restart it in the middle of the bay lest a broken fuel line cause a fire, so the officers volunteered to step down on the floats and paddle us to shore while I sat in the cockpit and steered against a slight crosswind with the water rudders.

As the paddles rhythmically swashed through the water on either side of the fuselage, I glanced about the large bay and humbly reflected on our fate had the problem arisen at a destination farther along on our itinerary: Point Baker, where an engine failure would have dropped us into the swells of Sumner Strait, or the fishing village at Meyers Chuck, where rocks lay at the end of the two principal takeoff paths.

The toes of the floats slid onto a gravely beach, and the officers replaced the paddles in their sheaths. I removed the top half of the cowling with a screwdriver from a small tool kit in the map compartment and studied the engine. There was no broken fuel line or injector or other obvious trouble. Next, with the clear plastic cup designed for the purpose I drained several ounces from all five fuel sumps—one in each wing tank, one in the engine, and two connected to lines under the fuselage. None of the samples contained water or sediment.

Then, with the toes of the floats still on the beach to hold the 185 in place, I started the engine. It ran normally with the auxiliary fuel pump off, indicating the engine-driven pump was functioning. "Well," I said, shaking my head, "everything seems to be okay. Let's give it another try." I assured the officers I would keep the airplane on the step for a few minutes before leaving the water to make sure the engine would continue running.

With the cowling refastened, we spun the 185 around and climbed in. So far I had not checked the engine instruments at full power; like many floatplane pilots, I took off by the seat of my pants and kept my eyes on the terrain for the first few seconds of climb. This time, however, I watched the gauges as I advanced the throttle.

All needles behaved until the final half inch of throttle travel, whereupon the fuel-flow needle swept right on by the red line into the manifold-pressure side of the dual instrument. The engine sputtered. I quickly yanked back the throttle, and we slowed to an idling taxi.

"Uh oh!" one of the officers exclaimed. But I felt relieved, for I now knew what ailed the engine: excess fuel at full power. Leaning the engine's fuel/air ratio with the mixture control seemed to be a reasonable remedy. After a successful step-taxi test, we took off and, carefully monitoring the fuel flow, returned to town with no further trouble.

In the office, Revilla owner Dale Clark grimaced as I related the events at Labouchere Bay. "I've heard of engines quitting because they didn't get enough fuel," he commented, "but I've never heard of one quitting at sea level because it got too much."

He and a mechanic explored the engine for several hours but found nothing amiss. The fuel filter showed no sign of contamination. Before putting everything back together, they adjusted the fuel flow down slightly for good measure.

The engine performed perfectly on a flight test, the fuel-flow needle dutifully pegging—and remaining—at the red line at full power. But no one felt satisfied. If the problem had been an excessive fuel-flow setting, why hadn't it manifested itself during the previous ten hours of flight? Why hadn't the engine quit on takeoff from Ketchikan or Bay of Pillars? We checked with other 185 pilots and mechanics in town and phoned several overhaul shops in the Seattle area; none had ever heard of an IO-520-D, or any engine, for that matter, flooding out on takeoff at sea level. A Continental factory representative also had no explanation.

The auxiliary fuel pump on a 185 was used in starting the engine and to provide a flow of fuel in case the engine-driven pump failed. In the "high" position the auxiliary fuel-pump switch was spring-loaded; the pilot had to hold his finger on it to maintain maximum pump operation. Had a temporary electrical short at Labouchere Bay turned on the pump at that position, we wondered? If the engine-driven pump was working, activation of the auxiliary pump would have caused an excessively rich fuel mixture—sort of like giving a full glass of Scotch to a party guest who had asked for two fingers' worth. We purposely kept the pump on high in a full-power test to see what would happen, but while the resulting overly rich mixture sent the fuel-flow needle slightly past the red line, it produced no power loss.

The possibility of pilot error undoubtedly arose in a few minds, and undoubtedly faded immediately. Other than deliberately holding the auxiliary fuel-pump switch in the high position during the takeoff run—an awkward act, which we had demonstrated probably would not have stopped the engine anyway—there simply was nothing a pilot could do at sea level to produce too much fuel on takeoff. At altitude, where the air was thinner and engines needed less fuel, failing to lean the mixture before applying full power could flood the engine. But Labouchere Bay's elevation was zero.

Nonetheless, I felt uncomfortable that Clark and the mechanic could not re-create the power loss and vindicate me. The incident remained a mystery, and the problem never recurred.

Afterward, I began choosing an emergency landing site before each takeoff. Just in case.

Besides feeling fortunate that my engine failure had happened over calm water rather than a hostile environment, I felt relieved that the incident had happened at all. While I rejected the superstition that some supernatural master plan alloted a certain number of mechanical woes to each pilot, I did trust the law of averages to insure me against further serious engine trouble. Few experienced pilots had had even one total engine failure, let alone two. Now that I had had mine, the likelihood of another in the next few years was statistically almost nil.

However, I was also aware that a flipped coin that landed heads up five consecutive times still had a fifty-fifty chance of landing heads up the sixth time.

When my next engine ordeal occurred, I had flown just 2000 additional hours, a relatively brief interlude. This time the culprit was human carelessness instead of an obscure mechanical gremlin. And the emergency lasted long enough for a large dose of terror.

I was in Juneau now after a year and a half in Seattle. Following three years with Revilla Flying Service, I had again left the frantic summers and the lean winters and the foggy passes of Southeast for a white-collar job with regular hours in a comfortable office. The Pacific Northwest had seemed to be an ideal compromise. It offered quick access to mountains, forests, waterways, and islands, just like Alaska. Seattle even had four water-based air services. People were friendly and relaxed. The weather was more civilized, the cost of living lower. Yet, there I could also find huge department stores, cultural events, squash courts—the variety of any large metropolitan area. Including jobs with a future.

For months I had rolled on the challenges and opportunities of my new career. Then, again, gradual monotony and boredom had brought disillusionment. And again I began to stare out the window and daydream about bush flying. Why could I not be content with the ordinary, relatively secure lifestyle that satisfied so many millions of other people? Did I have some constitutional need for adventure and insecurity? Hoping to regain spirit, I made my first parachute jump at a bucolic airport near Lake Sammamish in Issaquah. I also took a few glider lessons at the same facility, white-water rafted down the Suiattle River, and hiked on Washington state's highest mountain, 14,410-foot Mount Rainier.

But adventure in the Northwest seemed bland, like sailing on a lake instead of the ocean. Although the physical and mental demands could be as tough as I chose to make them, the atmosphere lacked romantic fire.

When I realized I was beginning to think seriously about returning to Alaska, I gulped. Hold on, here, I told myself. You've forsaken bush flying three times before for the sort of job you now hold. If you go back to the cockpit, do you really think you could avoid another bout of burnout? You remember the romance but forget the sweat and the rain. How much longer will the cycle continue? Your employment record in journalism is already unstable enough to make any interviewer frown. You can't keep leaving good jobs every several years and expect the door to remain open. You may already be in your last opportunity for a meaningful career. After this, you might have no option but to fly float-planes for the rest of your working life, changing companies as they furlough you or fold. Flying floatplanes in the Alaskan wilderness is not a skill that can be easily marketed elsewhere in the aviation industry, much less outside it. Even if you were young enough to be considered, the airlines would insist on a more appropriate aviation background.

Ten years earlier, tomorrow hadn't mattered. Life was for the present, to be experienced and enjoyed in pursuits of the heart. The future would take care of itself.

Now tomorrow did matter. I could see it in the mirror in the crow's-feet and receding hairline. I could see it in the simplicity of my tax returns. I could see it in the lonely, blank stares of the Seattle street people, who perhaps were lamenting lost opportunities as they held out their cups.

Despite these thoughts, the patient sirens of Alaska continued to whisper seductively. Odysseus had the foresight and discipline to stuff wax into his ears; I did not. When the lure became irresistible, I opted for Juneau and a change in routine.

Founded in 1880 on the site of a gold strike 210 miles up the archipelago from Ketchikan, Juneau was an exaggerated image of its perennial rival. It too was strung along a narrow channel, but with more buildings to accommodate its population of 25,600. The main road paralleled the waterfront with four lanes instead of two, and the mountains behind the city rose higher and more steeply. As the state capital, Juneau cost more and exuded an underlying snobbism compared with Ketchikan's red-neck ingenuousness.

But the two areas shared a need for air transportation; the bush around Juneau was equally roadless and bridgeless. With thirty employees and thirteen aircraft, my new company was the largest and oldest of Juneau's nine air services, the descendent of a one-airplane, one-man operation that part-owner Kenneth H. Loken founded in 1954. In addition to its waterfront facilities along Gastineau Channel, the company had an office at Juneau Municipal Airport, since some of the aircraft were amphibious. We berthed most of our floatplanes in a rectangular, man-made lake called the "pond" adjacent to the runway.

The airplanes were familiar to me, but not so most of the places the company served regularly: the Tlingit villages of Hoonah and Angoon, Tenakee Springs, the fishing hamlets of Elfin Cove and Pelican, the National Marine Fisheries Service's station at Little Port Walter, and others. For several days I flew in the right seat as an observer, then in the left as a pilot with a check pilot next to me, learning the routes. My experience in the Ketchikan area transferred readily to the process. While the beaches here were less rocky and glaciers gripped the steep mainland valleys like massive rivers of ice, the waterways, islands, and mountains imparted a sense of déjà vu; I quickly felt at home.

For tips on specific places, Loken, nicknamed "Pinky" for his perpetually ruddy complexion, could answer all questions. He often entered the waterfront operations room to check on the day's flights and, I suspected, to escape the paperwork drudgery in his office upstairs. No matter where inside a 100-mile radius of Juneau a pilot was bound, the tall, blond Loken had been there himself before retiring from the cockpit several years earlier. He would expound on special considerations, then, with sharp blue eyes that still needed no glasses after sixty-two years, tell an anecdote about one of his flights to the place. An avid hiker who had trekked in Nepal the year before, Loken talked about the bush with the wistful reverence of an aging adventurer.

But it was I who would have the adventure.

The first hint of trouble came from that mysterious inner voice some people call intuition. The dispatcher had scheduled me to fly N5603R on Tuesday, after the Cessna 206 came out of the hangar for a routine

100-hour inspection. When the mechanics did a compression check at the end of the inspection that morning, however, they found four of the six cylinders below limits. That meant another couple of days in the shop for the airplane. I spent the time getting settled in my new home; most of the company's aircraft had yet to come out of winter storage, and with just ten days of employment, I had to yield other available airplanes to pilots with more seniority.

The mechanics worked late into the night on Wednesday, and Thursday morning I was pleased to find N5603R cowled outside the hangar. But when we carted it over to the seaplane elevator, we discovered the tide was too low to get it into the water. Noon would be the soonest the incoming tide would reach the lower end of the elevator's runners.

"This airplane just doesn't want to go to work," I muttered as the mechanics and I stared down at the algae-coated bottom of the elevator frame. Made in jest, the comment seemed to hang ominously in the air for minutes afterward.

The foreboding haunted me again later that morning at the airport terminal, where I wiled away the hours with the land-based air taxi people. As we sipped coffee, someone with a radio scanner suddenly turned up the volume. A Canadian Super Cub on wheels that had left Juneau for Atlin, British Columbia, had encountered freezing rain up the Taku Inlet and was limping back to the airport. Again and again we heard the pilot radio the tower that he was going to crash-land because of a loss of power, only to announce in a shaky voice a few seconds later that "the engine has come up now."

In a morbid way there was something humorous in the repetition of this cycle. Most of the dozen pilots, dispatchers, and passengers who had gathered around the scanner chuckled in unison at each status change. I started to smile with the crowd but felt instantly guilty. Somehow, I shared the pilot's lonely desperation, a sensation that clouded my anticipation of flying even after he landed safely at the airport.

With 03R finally in the water, the dispatcher assigned me to make a 1 P.M. flight to the villages of Tenakee Springs and Angoon and a cabin at Gambier Bay. After leveling off at 1500 feet at the north end of Douglas Island by the airport and throttling back to cruise power, I noticed that the fuel-flow gauge read fourteen gallons per hour instead of the usual sixteen. Since the other engine instruments were giving normal indications, I concluded the gauge simply needed adjustment. I would so inform the mechanics when I returned to Juneau.

At Tenakee, a hot-springs resort community of eighty by Tenakee Inlet on Chichagoff Island, I dropped off a passenger and a load of mail and freight. While taxiing out I twice had to give the engine a spurt of power to keep it from dying. Idle set too low. I'd mention that, too.

The fuel flow read just twelve gallons per hour during the climb-out from Tenakee, and the needle slowly sank until it pegged at zero over Chatham Strait. The rest of the engine instruments continued to report healthy vital signs. Obviously, the fuel-flow gauge was broken. Occasionally the smell of fuel wafted into my nostrils now, but I assumed the odor lingered from a chain saw I had unloaded at Tenakee.

As I worked my way across the strait and down the west coast of Admiralty Island toward Angoon, sleet and a gusty east wind began thrashing 03R: the edge of a front forecast to arrive in the Juneau area later that day. The wind, whipping the water into three-foot waves off Admiralty, forced me to crab thirty degrees toward the shore to maintain a straight track. Fighting the gusts with constant input to the ailerons and rudder, I splashed down to a landing in the harbor at the Tlingit Indian village.

The engine quit when I throttled back to taxi. "Damn this idle!" I mumbled, restarting the engine. At the dock I unloaded my remaining two passengers—who had been sitting behind me in the two middle seats—and the rest of the mail and freight. The company's Angoon agent later told the dispatcher in Juneau he thought the engine sounded rough when I took off.

My last stop was on the east side of Admiralty at Gambier Bay, where a man and his wife had radioed for transportation to Juneau from their cabin. The sleet and scud blocked the passes across the island, so I continued down the shoreline, intending to follow the water all the way around.

But I paid little attention to the weather now. The airspeed indicator was oscillating between just 85 and 90 knots in the turbulence, although the 206 was empty of payload weight and I had set the power for normal cruise. The needle should have been wavering between 110 and 115 knots. Was the airspeed indicator also breaking down? And was the engine rasping slightly, like someone who ought to clear his throat? And that fuel smell! I advanced the prop control and throttle to climb power, but the airspeed needle rose to only 100 knots.

For a minute I tried to convince myself that the below-normal airspeed resulted from offshore downdrafts that were forcing me to fly with a nose-up attitude, and that the engine roughness was actually the slipstream whistling through tiny window or door spaces. As a new pilot in Juneau, I was eager to prove my worth by completing assignments. I wanted to avoid an early reputation for turning back because of minor or imaginary mechanical trouble.

But pretending could not mask the evidence of a growing problem. It could not change the proper professional response. With a curse, I banked away from the shoreline to begin a turn back toward Juneau. As I glanced out the right window to watch the murky horizon during the turn, the corner of my eye noticed liquid sloshing on the floor in the foot well of the right-hand seat. Dripping passenger boots flashed into my mind and vanished immediately—boots could not have deposited that much fluid. Knowing what I would learn, I reached over, stuck my finger in, and smelled.

Fuel!

The specter of a sudden inferno sent adrenaline tingling through my veins and nearly strangled me with claustrophobia. I was now abeam Chaik Bay, just ten miles south of Angoon. But I had no faith in the engine to get me back to the village, or even to a sheltered cove in Chaik Bay. If I headed for one of those sanctuaries against the fierce wind and the engine suddenly quit or blew up, I would come down on the windward side of Chatham Strait to drift helplessly away from land into increasingly rough water that would almost certainly capsize the airplane and sap the life from me. With the wind on my tail, however, I could quickly cross the eight-mile-wide strait to the downwind side, the east shore of Baranof Island. There I would at least drift toward land.

Frowning through the windshield, I turned 03R toward the outline of Baranof, barely visible through the sleet. I shut off all electrical equipment and pushed the control wheel forward until the airplane was about twenty feet above the waves. Now I could plant the floats onto the water and dive out in case the cockpit erupted in flames. Then I fiddled with my fingers beneath the seat until I unlatched the fire extinguisher and placed the cylinder in my lap. Although the airplane had six life jackets, I never thought to slip into one.

My pounding heart seemed to spur the airplane on. I reached Baranof in less than four minutes and turned north, staying close to both the water and shoreline. My chart showed the nearest habitation on this side to be back at Tenakee, some thirty miles away. Should I land in the first protected cove while the engine was still running, beach the airplane as best I could and wait? Search aircraft would scour Admiralty Island first; it would be at least tomorrow afternoon before someone would check this stretch of Baranof. And the wind was forecast to increase to forty knots or higher in the evening.

As I watched the swells smash against the rocks and reefs, spraying the trunks of the spruce and hemlock trees cluttering the banks, I felt an overwhelming urge to let someone know what was happening. I hesitated, then pressed the dual battery/alternator master switch and cringed against an explosion. The engine rasped on. Next, I gingerly flicked on the avionics master switch and cringed again.

In recent years the FAA had installed remote-communication-outlet repeater stations on strategically located mountaintops to enhance radio communications in mountainous Southeast. Thus, despite my extremely low altitude, I pulled the microphone off its hook and called the Juneau Flight Service Station. Silence. I twirled the knobs on the radio to 121.5 megahertz, the universal mayday frequency, and transmitted in the blind. Again there was no response. Since I was unaware of the locations of the RCO repeater-station sites in this part of the region, I began trying RCO frequencies at random. The fourth frequency I tuned in was 121.4 MHz.

"Cessna Five Six Zero Three Romeo, this is Sitka Radio, go ahead."

The voice was a puff of air in an airless box, although of course the speaker could do nothing to mend the ailing engine or defuse the leaking fuel. I explained the situation, said I was going to try to make Tenakee and asked the specialist to notify the company. Every few minutes thereafter his voice entered my earphones to ask my position and estimated time of arrival at Tenakee. I fretted over the answers because the country was new to me and I was flying so close to the surface that the shoreline blocked from my view many of the features depicted on my chart. But by dead reckoning and following my progress with my finger on the chart like a poor reader working through a paragraph, I managed to keep track of my position.

At the mouths of bays, where I had to leave the security of the shoreline for a minute or more, I coaxed the engine with the plea, "Come on, come on, keep going!" until I was again within gliding distance of the shoreline.

Although I was reluctant to have the information, I also kept track of the growing pool of fuel on the right-hand floor. I leaned over periodically to watch spurts shoot out from the upper firewall area like milk from a cow, splashing on the floor. I tried mopping up the pool with paper towels, but I quickly exhausted the roll. The effort was academic, anyway; the danger from leaking fuel lay not on the floor, where there was no source of ignition, but in the engine and accessories area, which was fraught with intense heat, electrical wiring, and possibly sparks.

If the engine suddenly exploded, would the cockpit be instantly engulfed in fire, or would the firewall contain the flames long enough for me to ditch? I had already opened all the air vents within reach to dispel the fuel odor. Now I shut them to prevent the rush of air from fanning the flames I might have to face.

The falling needles on the fuel gauges showed about twice the normal consumption for the eighty minutes I had been in the air. The bad-weather forecast and my unfamiliarity with this part of Southeast had inspired me to pump twenty gallons into the right tank as a reserve. Those twenty gallons now seemed like liquid gold; without them I would be unable to reach Tenakee.

I frowned each time I glanced at the climb-power settings on the manifold pressure and tachometer gauges. Throttling back to cruise power would reduce the fuel consumption and perhaps also lower the rate of fuel leakage. But I might unwittingly have selected the one power combination that, for reasons beyond my understanding of mechanics, chemistry, and physics, had thus far inhibited an explosion. Throttling back might change things and prompt a sudden boom—or a sudden silence up front. I opted for the status quo.

Just beyond Basket Bay I finally flew back out of the sleet. The gusty wind persisted, but my spirits rose with the visibility and ceiling. As my chances of making Tenakee increased, so did my eagerness to get there. I began fidgeting, grinding my teeth, and glancing at the panel clock, which seemed to show only a few seconds' advance for each minute I believed had passed.

At last I rounded the southern corner of Tenakee Inlet and gained a tailwind. Several minutes later I turned upwind to land in front of the quaint community.

"Sitka, Zero Three Romeo, landing Tenakee. Thanks for your help," I said into the mike. There was no answer; the mountains along Tenakee Inlet blocked the communications facilities that had relayed our previouis transmissions.

Roiled by the wind, the water glared with dark, angry waves. But the 206 had electric flaps, and I debated only a second before deciding not to risk a spark by deploying them. I held the floats off the waves as long as possible to dissipate the excess speed of a no-flaps approach and made a full-stall landing. The airplane shuddered from the jolt and bounced several times before falling off the step.

The engine quit. I restarted it twice before reaching the dock. There, the company's waiting Tenakee agent, whom the dispatcher had notified of my problem, grabbed the wing strut and pulled the plane to the bumpers.

"Got a little engine trouble, huh?" he said. The air smelled fresh and delicious as we walked up the ramp to the Snyder Mercantile Company, the local general store, and I breathed deeply of it. After a long drink of water, I called the company, asked the dispatcher to inform the FAA that I had landed safely, and gave details of the flight to a mechanic. Then I went back outside and strolled along Tenakee's narrow, graveled street, savoring the wind in my face and the crunch of pebbles beneath my boots. An elderly hunchbacked woman shuffled by, acknowledging me with only a faint smile. Residents were used to visiting tourists, fishermen, and hunters. To her I was just another stranger, undeserving of special attention. Fuel leaks and faltering aircraft engines were beyond her knowledge or concern. Life went on.

By the time another company 206 landed with a mechanic an hour later, sleet had begun to pelt the little community. Zero Three Romeo promptly dispelled whatever superstition I had harbored that its woes would mysteriously disappear the moment the mechanic arrived. As I taxied the airplane around to the other side of the dock to run it up on the seaplane ramp so the mechanic could work on it, the engine quit four times, and the backfiring sounded like a gun battle. Mechanic Clyde Dammel and pilot Jacques Norvell stood solemnly on the dock, watching and listening.

After Dammel removed the top half of 03R's cowling, Norvell and I placed it into the other 206 to keep the wind from blowing it off the dock. Dammel needed just a few moments to locate the trouble. Two fuel lines, he candidly told us, had been left untightened when he and the other mechanics had worked late the night before to complete the 100-hour inspection. Both lines had gradually vibrated loose during my flight. One served the fuel-flow instrument and was the source of the fuel leaking into the cockpit. The fuel had gathered behind the firewall and spilled through openings onto the floor in spurts as it sloshed around. Meanwhile, the untightened fuel-injector line to the number five cylinder had caused the power loss when it worked itself off.

It had sprayed raw fuel continuously over the hot engine.

I contemplated the news and its considerations:

If one of my Angoon passengers had sat in the right front seat, he would have noticed the leaking fuel and alerted me, allowing me to terminate the flight much sooner. Whenever I had passengers, the right front seat was almost always occupied. But these two had asked to sit in the middle seats, leaving the one next to me empty.

If I had had a load of passengers or freight after leaving Angoon, climb power probably would have been insufficient to stay in the air. A higher setting would have meant more fuel and more heat. Would it also have meant an explosion, or fuel exhaustion before Tenakee?

If I had been more familiar with the Juneau area, I would have taken on much less of a fuel reserve at Juneau, which would have put Tenakee beyond 03R's range, under the circumstances.

I had thought the fire danger came solely from the source that was leaking fuel onto the floor, which actually posed relatively little threat. Had I been aware of the far more serious leak from the loose injector line, I probably would have ditched the airplane as soon as I reached the Baranof shoreline—and thus lost the airplane and possibly my life.

Dammel reattached and secured the two fuel lines and replaced the cowling, and I mopped up the pool of fuel on the floor with paper towels from the other 206. There was still enough fuel in 03R for the twenty-five-minute flight to Juneau. Norvell took off in his airplane and Dammel accompanied me to be on hand in case further trouble developed. We made the flight in silence, the airspeed now at 115 knots and the engine droning heartily. As we taxied toward the dock in town, I turned to Dammel.

"What could I have done to reduce the fire risk?"

Dammel grimaced and shook his head. "Not a thing. You were one damn lucky pilot. It should have ignited."

ICE CAP BLUES

▼▲▼▲▼▲▼▲▼▲▼▲▼▲▼▲▼▲▼▲▼▲▼▲▼▲▼▲▼▲▼▲▼▲▼▲▼▲▲

How high is sea level up here?" the woman in the right front seat yelled above the engine roar of the Beaver as we climbed out from Gastineau Channel. She appeared to be in her fifties, a heavy person with bushy gray hair, glasses, and a southern accent. At first I thought she was joking, and I started to smile in appreciation. But her deadpan, expectant expression told me the question was serious.

The woman and five other passengers from the cruise ship *Daphne* were aboard the Beaver for a tour of the nearby Juneau ice cap, a spectacular mass of ice and snow covering 1500 square miles and spawning some three dozen glaciers. It was mid-May, and although I had begun flying commercially in Juneau a month earlier, this was my first ice cap flight; the cruise ships were just starting their seasonal voyages up the Inside Passage. For the next four months the ships, sometimes three or four in the harbor at once, would deliver up to 4000 tourists to the capital city virtually every day. Depending on the weather, dozens or hundreds would sign up for a tour of the ice cap. Besides flying to the usual bush places, we served as tour guides.

"How high is sea level up here?" the woman yelled again, apparently interpreting my hesitation to mean I hadn't heard her initially.

"Well, ma'am," I yelled back, trying not to sound derisive, "sea level is the same all over the world, whether it's the Arctic Ocean or the South Pacific."

"Oh."

I wanted to pick up the microphone and share the woman's ignorance with my fellow pilots, whose aircraft were strung out in a loose line at various altitudes behind me en route to the ice cap. But I knew that several of them—and thus their passengers—were listening over the speaker instead of through headphones. So, I diplomatically waited until we returned to the Juneau Seadrome downtown, unloaded our passengers, and gathered in the office at the top of the ramp for the next group. Then I discovered the joke was on me.

"Hell, we all hear that question about ten times a summer," chuckled one pilot who had flown in Juneau for several years. "You won't believe some of the questions these cruise ship people ask you."

I became a believer a few days later when an elderly man sitting behind me tapped my shoulder as we entered Taku Inlet.

"What kind of fish are those down there?" he shouted at my headphones.

I glanced below, curious. It was too early in the Season for salmon jumpers; had he spotted a pod of whales or porpoises? "Where?" I twisted my neck to look at the man.

The man shook his head slightly and scowled at my lack of observation. "There! All over! Don't you see them?" Then, watching me scan the water without success, he added, "Those white fish, jumping everywhere!"

Suddenly I understood. "Ah, those are whitecaps, sir."

"Whitecaps—are they good to eat?"

Another tourist asked if I would circle the North Pole for him. The ice cap may have resembled his image of the top of the world, but I would have had to fly several thousand miles to comply. Two tourists also asked me to fly by an Eskimo village so they could take pictures of igloos to show the folks back home. I explained that Southeast had no Eskimo villages, that most Eskimos in the state resided in western and Arctic Alaska, hundreds of miles from Juneau, and that they lived in buildings, like non-native Alaskans. And many tourists wanted to take a look at the trans-Alaska oil pipeline, the closest portion of which lay at Valdez, almost 500 miles to the northwest.

One of our pilots swore a tourist once asked him deadpan where she could exchange dollars for Alaskan currency. Another pilot claimed he got a request to point out penguins.

But most questions on ice cap tours over the next several months were more routine. And repetitious. A dollar for each, "Why is the ice blue?" would have enabled me to buy my own cruise ship and sail for Tahiti. (Glacial ice becomes prismatic from compression and reflects blue but absorbs other colors of the light spectrum.) Dozens of tourists were also eager to find out how many trips a day I made to the ice cap; they seemed surprised to learn the company flew to camps, villages, lakes, and other destinations as well and that many days I didn't get to the ice cap at all.

And dozens wanted to know if I *ever* got tired of giving aerial tours of such magnificent scenery. The easiest answer was a simple smile and shake of the head. In my mind, however, I silently gave a different answer: Well, ma'am, I too marveled at the sights on my first ten or fifteen tours, but now, after fifty or sixty I find the ice cap a bit monotonous, especially on days when I have to make back-to-back tours and answer the same questions again and again.

After a day of ice cap tours, we all ached for the blessed variety of charters and the seasoned sophistication of bush residents.

Most tourists had never been in a floatplane, or in any aircraft smaller than a 727, so many questions concerned safety: "Do you have enough gas, young man?" "Are you sure this thing is safe?" "You *do* have a license, don't you?" Gradually, the endless repetition of such unnecessary questions prompted me to reply with sarcasm: "No, sir, we have only enough fuel to get us halfway there." "I don't know; I've never been up in it before." "Yes, indeed, I've had a license since Thursday."

Interestingly, sarcasm seemed to relax the tourists more than straight answers. Still, I frequently saw apprehension in their eyes when, taxiing out for takeoff, I turned around to brief them on the flight. Smiling reassured some, but others, like overimaginative children lying in bed listening to every creak in the house, looked for apparent discrepancies to challenge me with. Many tourists noticed the permanent mooring lines on the floats while we taxied and urgently informed me that I had forgotten to "take off those ropes" before leaving the dock. And because the doors on airliners are closed before taxiing begins, countless tourists interrupted my briefing to tell me I had neglected to close the cockpit door of the floatplane. Tourists continued to so enlighten me even after I started holding the door two feet open with my elbow to show obvious intention. Eventually, I typed up the following card, laminated it, and carried it in my shirt pocket to whip out and present with a smile to whoever broached the question:

ICE CAP BLUES

To avoid the tedium of answering other frequent comments or questions over and over, I began adding to my briefing the half-truth that the engine was too loud for a talking tour. I passed out ice cap informational brochures the company had prepared and asked the passengers to hold their questions until we landed back in Juneau—realizing that by then some questions would be forgotten.

While it was possible to shout out facts about the scenery en route, particularly in the Cessnas, the pilot had to repeat them several times before everyone heard, a tiring, voice-straining effort. Audible comments also required the pilot to talk over his shoulder, a potentially dangerous distraction with up to a dozen other sightseeing aircraft in the area.

Just as some airline passengers ignore the flight attendants' instructions about fastening seatbelts, however, some tourists asked the usual questions while we were airborne anyway. A few refused to be discouraged. I would say, "I beg your pardon?" The tourist would ask again. "I'm sorry, I still didn't hear you." The tourist would lean toward me and patiently repeat the question. I'd wait a moment as if trying to understand, then remove my headphones, exaggerating the effort, and cock my head. "One more time, please." Finally, I'd answer the question, hoping I'd made my point. But after a few minutes of peace other persistent questions would follow:

149

"How cold does it get in the winter up here?" "How deep are those cracks?" (cravasses). "How thick is the ice?" etc., etc.

One man, who said he was a retired engineer from Missouri, even tried to carry on a conversation during the flight. The thundering 450-horsepower Beaver engine drowned most of his words, and I quickly stopped trying to participate. He continued with an inaudible monologue. To be polite, I periodically nodded and smiled at him.

Yet, with some passengers I risked laryngitis and volunteered comments. An attractive woman, for example. And the occasional celebrities or VIPs who stepped off the ships to fly with us: Frank Borman, the astronaut and Eastern Air Lines president; Mayor Tom Bradley of Los Angeles; several professional football players; a fabulously wealthy Saudi Arabian prince who chartered a separate airplane to transport his servants; actor George Kennedy; the late actress Gloria Swanson; and others.

Some more humble groups also cajoled comments out of me by ooing and ahhing at the ice cap with infectious enthusiasm. One delightful Oklahoma couple began uttering exclamations about less spectacular, nonglacial Southeast scenery long before we reached the ice cap. They gaped in wide-eyed astonishment when the glaciers became visible.

Like most tourists, they clicked the shutters on their cameras furiously as we passed nunataks, cirques, icefalls, and other features. Even though the brilliant sunshine had forced me to wear sunglasses against the glare, they used flashes.

At the other end of the scale, I occasionally had passengers who seemed unimpressed. They sat glumly, yawned, glanced at their watches, and pulled out a paperback. The boredom prize went to a middle-aged man who napped against his window during the flight, his glasses sliding down his nose from the vibration. He had paid seventy dollars for the ice cap tour.

Along with the odd blank expressions were a few complaints. Many of the elderly, overweight, or lame passengers grumbled about their struggle to get in and out of the plane. With narrow steps inclined at a steep angle on the float struts and cabins cramped with closely spaced seats, the Cessnas and Beavers were indeed hostile to the less agile. Once in, some were unable to arise from the seat after landing and had to be pulled up. Others could ride only in one of the larger, twin-engine Gooses, which had a door at dock level and an aisle in the cabin.

After living in pampered luxury on the cruise ships, the tourists perhaps expected to step into a big, turbine-powered Twin Otter with a pair of pilots in snappy uniforms who would narrate the tour over a public-address system complete with individual headphones. Instead, they got a spartan, noisy floatplane with a single, blue-jean-clad pilot who flew mostly in silence. Welcome to Alaska, folks. You're not in Greenwich anymore.

Other passengers were disappointed in the lack of visible wildlife on their flight. "I didn't see *one* animal!" snapped a man after we landed from a tour. Travel brochures and books that trumpeted Alaska's wildlife but neglected to mention that much of it was concealed by terrain or foliage gave some visitors to the state the impression they would see great herds of beasts covering the slopes and meadows, à la Seregenti Plain.

Of course, often we did spot a moose, bear, or mountain goat along the Taku River valley bordering the ice cap. Several times after I descended and circled an animal, the cabin erupted in delighted applause. A tip usually followed back at the dock in Juneau. Other pilots reported the same reaction, and we half-seriously discussed placing stuffed animals along the route.

Some tourists also complained because clouds or rain obscured part of the scenery — although usually they had signed up for the tour in similar conditions back in town an hour before. With each ice cap seat bringing seventy dollars, the company was understandably loathe to ground the sightseeing squadron just because the weather prevented us from climbing 4000 feet to get up on the ice cap itself. Most tourists, the company realized, were not repeat customers. As long as we could fly safely in the Taku River valley below the ice cap, the green light was on. The Norris, Hole-in-the-Wall, Taku, West Twin, and East Twin glaciers descended to the valley floor, so even if we couldn't climb above 500 feet, we could still give our passengers a detailed look at the termini of those glaciers. The calved icebergs, crevasses, morraine deposits, and icefalls were especially fascinating up close. And flying low gave passengers a better chance to spot wildlife and examine the lush valley scenery.

Pilots heard the comment, "This has been the highlight of our trip to Alaska!" almost as often after low-altitude, bad-weather tours as on clear days when we could climb high. Besides, we rationalized, tourists on low-altitude tours didn't know what they were missing above, hidden in the clouds.

Still, we admitted to one another that the tourists were being misled, if not cheated, when an ice cap tour lacked a look at the actual ice cap. We flew the tours in bad weather without protest because that was our job (and, for some pilots, because their pay was strictly by the flight hour). To ease our consciences, some of us advised the passengers before takeoff that while the weather did not permit an ice cap tour per se, much spectacular scenery awaited their eyes, anyway.

The practice of sending out sightseeing flights in nonsightseeing weather was fairly universal among Southeast operators. In Ketchikan, where the local attraction was Misty Fjords National Monument, my fellow pilots and I gave many "tours" in visibility that restricted us to weaving along the shorelines of the fjords at 200 feet; the passengers saw nothing of the monument's magnificent valleys, lakes, and peaks. But the company made lots of money.

With rain and tendrils of fog cutting visibility and restricting aircraft to the Taku River valley, we worried more about a midair collision than satisfying the customers. We monitored the same frequency on our radios during ice cap tours and, in bad weather, turned on our landing lights and transmitted periodic position/altitude reports: "Eight-seven-three passing Grizzly Flats at 700." In fair weather, however, the radios crackled mostly with chit-chat, even though FAA statistics consistently showed that collisions nationwide occurred mostly in sunshine: "Anybody see any moose down there?" "Only six more hours and we can go home." "Hey Roger, you going back to Louisiana for the winter?"

Some tours included a stop at a renovated log cabin called the Taku Lodge on the Taku River, where the passengers ate a salmon dinner, gazed at the glacial scenery, and walked on short nature trails. If we had no intervening flights, we waited for them. Most of us migrated to the kitchen. There we drank coffee, chatted, played cards, and swatted the mosquitoes that somehow managed to find a way into the room despite the screens protecting the windows and back door. With luck, there would be leftover king salmon filets, baked beans, jello, sourdough rolls, and cookies for us after the tourists had their dinner ("pilot food," according to the kitchen helpers). While we ate, we occasionally saw a bear prowling across the grass by the outbuildings, scrounging for its own leftover meal.

On particularly busy days when the schedule permitted no such breaks, we left our passengers at the lodge for another flight back in town and returned for them later. One afternoon, after delivering some fishermen to a lake, I scooted back to the lodge to retrieve a load of tourists. As I taxied in I saw that the other aircraft had taken up most of the dock; only a small section between a Goose and a Beaver was left. On salt water or a lake there would have been insufficient room to glide in to the spot. But with the river racing downstream and the nose of the 206 pointed upstream, I could apply just enough power to offset the current, then use the water rudders to slip sideways into the slot at zero forward speed. The maneuver would require finesse, but I had done it before in similar circumstances.

A couple of pilots stood on the dock ready to secure the airplane to a cleat when the float reached the bumpers. About forty waiting tourists watched in a cluster on the bank of the river. Closer and closer I inched the 206 toward its berth. Ah, observe the great master execute this neat procedure, everybody! Another ten yards now.

Suddenly, the two pilots pointed toward the tail and motioned with their hands. I turned to look just as the right stabilizer hooked the Goose's left wing-float strut. In the strong current the 206 instantly pivoted toward the Goose. I quickly switched off the magnetoes, killing the engine. The prop stopped a second before the 206 slammed against the bow of the larger plane.

I scrambled out the door and climbed onto the wings of the 206, and several other pilots climbed on top of the Goose. An inspection indicated just minor damage in the form of dents and scrapes to both aircraft. But how to separate the planes? The current held the 206 against the Goose as if they were welded together. The teenager the lodge employed as a lineboy rushed to the boat shed and returned two minutes later with a skiff. He attached a line to the 206 and gunned the outboard, but the planes stubbornly held their embrace.

Meanwhile, the solemn, silent audience on the bank continued to watch the show while they slapped at mosquitoes.

The Goose was the farthest downstream airplane at the dock. It finally occurred to us that if we simply untied the Goose and released it into the river with the 206, the force of the current would be negated and the aircraft would easily separate. I climbed back into the 206 and the Goose pilot got into his plane. Someone untied the lines of the Goose, and the river swept us away. Moments later we drifted apart.

We had already agreed that once separated, both aircraft would return to town without passengers for a more thorough inspection by the mechanics. After my takeoff, I was tempted instead to head for the most remote wilderness lake I could find and hide from the world. The passing days gradually soothed my ego. When another pilot got tangled up with a Beaver in a similar docking mishap three weeks later, I slapped him on the back and welcomed him to the club.

In late September the last cruise ship of the Season sailed out of Juneau down the Inside Passage toward the Lower Forty-eight, and the infamous Taku winds soon began roaring across the ice cap. Most of our flights now went to bush destinations. Virtually all of our passengers were resident Southeasterners, who were much less troublesome than the tourists. There was just one catch:

The local folks never tipped.

ENDICOTT VISION

You're on prime time TV, so make a good landing!" Correspondent Geraldo Rivera, then with ABC's "20/20," grinned at me from the right seat of the Cessna 206. The program was about to shoot a segment on the logging camp at Coffman Cove on the northeastern end of Prince of Wales Island. The camera crew had flown out the day before and planned to film Rivera's arrival by floatplane. In addition to the technicians, I could see a couple of dozen camp residents on the seaplane dock below, waiting and watching.

"Thanks for the pressure!" I quipped to Rivera, a vivacious, charismatic man with a thick mustache and an easy smile. A brisk east wind stirred the air and the water, but I managed to set the airplane down with reasonable smoothness.

"We'll give you an A minus," he said.

He asked me to dock on the right side of the airplane so he could step out first for the cameras. A rainshower had moved through the area minutes before. With the crew capturing the scene and the sound, Rivera clambered out, grinned at camp spokesperson Leeta Valentine, slipped on the wet dock, and fell hard on his buttocks.

"Shit!" he exclaimed.

He climbed back into the cockpit, and I restarted the engine and taxied around for take two. This time he stayed on his feet and was greeted again by Leeta Valentine.

Rivera told the Southeast media that "20/20" intended the segment to be a simple study of life in a logging camp, but skeptical Southeasterners chewed their fingernails for weeks. The program often featured scathing investigative reports, and Coffman Cove had two reasons to be a target: the camp had been built practically on top of a 4000-year-old archeological site, and clearcut logging was a controversial practice many conservationists wanted to ban. However, when the segment finally aired, a record Southeast audience sighed in relief to see that it was indeed an innocent lifestyle study.

Although I had played a minor role, I watched the show with less concentration than most viewers. A week earlier, a former journalism colleague from New York had phoned to announce that he had been named editor-in-chief of a new aviation magazine to be published in Washington, D.C. It would be a slick publication with the highest quality articles, photos, and advertisers. Sure to become the standard by which other aviation magazines were judged. A great opportunity for everyone involved. And the position of senior editor was unfilled.

As I watched myself on the screen touch down at Coffman Cove with Rivera, my mind again trudged through long-familiar arguments, pro and con. On one side: a temporarily unlocked door I had thought would remain welded shut forever, a final chance for a respectable career that would open other intriguing doors along the way. I could start out high on the ladder and be absorbed instantly in responsibility, challenges, and creativity. On the other side: continued enmeshment in a life of aerial adventure, with its unpredictable, inexhaustible supply of excitement and color.

King Solomon would have torn out his hair trying to judge which was the wisest course. Emotionally drained by the debate, I could only crawl into bed, hoping that I'd awaken with an epiphany-like decision. But, as usual, the morning brought vacillation.

I remained in limbo three days later as I flew into the mouth of Muir Inlet, sixty-five miles northwest of Juneau in the northeastern part of Glacier Bay National Park. I had just dropped off well-known Juneau film maker Joel Bennett and an assistant to shoot a documentary on mountain goats in the park. Now I was heading for the mouth of the Endicott River over by Lynn Canal to pick up a company mechanic and his wife. Planning a lazy day of beachcombing and picnicking, the couple had hitched a ride to the river early that morning on a company Beaver bound for Haines at the head of the canal.

Glacier Bay, a 4981-square-mile world of ice, mountains, and inlets, was a sightseer's dream. Off the left wing, the ice of Muir Glacier extended upslope to Mount Harris. The late-afternoon sun had already dipped behind the Saint Elias Mountain Range to the west, stripping the ice of the golden coat it had worn earlier but leaving shadows to enhance its turquoise tint. Mount Fairweather, Southeast's highest mountain at 15,300 feet, towered there like an icy behemoth. Along the banks of Adams Inlet ahead, moraine deposits from retreating glaciers resembled sand dunes. Scattered stands of trees and shrubbery poked through the fringes of the otherwise barren mounds.

Cursing silently, I forced myself to put on mental blinders. Tomorrow I had to phone the editor-in-chief of the new Washington, D.C., magazine and inform him whether we would become colleagues again. Although the answer I would give was currently as much of a mystery to me as to him, I had at least come to a vital preliminary resolution: I would make up my damn mind one way or the other on this portion of the flight, while I had no passengers. By the time I picked up the mechanic and his wife, the decision would be final. No matter what. Period. With the mouth of the Endicott River just twenty-five minutes away, I could afford no time for sightseeing.

But the scenery refused to be ignored, for it figured in the debate—on both sides. Returning to a city office would mean renouncing wonders such as these around me. The Washington Monument and the Lincoln Memorial could hardly compensate. Yet, the local scenery included more than mountains and glaciers. A few miles behind me, a small cruise ship sliced through the water by Drake Island. I had noticed it while descending for a landing with Bennett and his assistant. It might have been the *Glacier Seal*, the *Thunder Bay*, or one of several other cruise ships that regularly brought tourists to Glacier Bay. More important than the name was the implication of the vessel's presence.

Each year I had flown in Southeast I had carried more sightseeing tourists than the year before, and transported more sportsmen to a growing number of resorts. The tiny, roadless fishing hamlet of Elfin Cove alone, forty miles to the south on Chichagof Island, now had three resorts. The visiting dudes there sometimes threatened to outnumber the year-round population of fifty.

Many outsiders were coming to stay. In fact, Alaska was now the fastest growing state in the country, and no longer the least populated one; Wyoming had recently taken over that distinction. While the Alaskan business community applauded the state's new ranking, many common folk like me had viewed the news with the same somber meditation that Vermonters probably engaged in when they learned the Green Mountain state no longer had more cows than people.

The "20/20" segment would attract more newcomers. So would the documentary Bennett planned. Ditto a nationwide TV advertising campaign the state's Division of Tourism had launched. While the growth rate would fluctuate with the fortunes of industries like oil, the arrow would probably always point up. Population growth is only one ingredient in that dubious broth called progress, of which all civilizations inevitably drink. As the moraine deposits along Adams Inlet gave way to the forest and slopes of the Chilkat Mountains, I pondered the other changes I had seen since I first came to Alaska fifteen years earlier—changes I had helped bring about by transporting the people responsible for them.

Ketchikan had had some planked streets and sidewalks then. Now it had none. The Haida village of Hydaburg then had sat isolated on the shores of Sukkwan Strait. Now a 21.6-mile gravel road connected it to the Hollis-Craig road, and thus to the Hollis ferry terminal. The Hollis-Craig road itself had been gravel. Now vehicles drove on black pavement there. Swan Lake on Revillagigedo Island had radiated wilderness peace and beauty. Now, logged and dammed, it emitted a different aura as part of Ketchikan's hydroelectric system. Bush residents had spent idle hours engrossed in reading or creative arts. Now, many lounged in front of satellite-based color TV sets.

I had seen changes in aviation, too.

Floatplanes had lost a little of their omnipresence with construction of airports at Ketchikan, Kake, Klawock, and Hoonah. Especially in northern Southeast, many pilots—both commercial and private—had switched from floats to wheels to save operational costs.

Skyrocketing insurance rates had forced a number of air taxis into mergers or bankruptcy.

Traditional high-frequency radios had become obsolete because of the expansion of the better-quality very-high-frequency facilities.

New Loran C radios for airplanes, with which some pilots were experimenting, had promised to revolutionize bad-weather navigation.

The FAA had cracked down on rule-breakers, both individual and commercial; my company in Juneau had paid a stiff fine for maintenance violations.

Many outfits had computerized their reservations and bookkeeping systems, and the larger ones had added turbine-powered airplanes to their fleets.

In the offing, under a national FAA flight service station consolidation program, was the reduction of Alaska's twenty-seven FSSs to three. Juneau would be the site of the Southeast regional station. When the network of communications-relay facilities was completed, pilots anywhere in Southeast supposedly would be able to contact an FSS specialist at Juneau by remote control to file a flight plan, check the weather, or call for help.

What other electronic, computerized progress did the future hold for bush flying? Would the outlying communities one day have navigational systems that would let pilots fly to them on instruments, and to hell with the fog? Would bush pilots eventually become airborne computer operators like modern airline pilots, following rigid routes, altitudes, and procedures in a prison of regimentation? Would the lumbering Beaver with its old-fashioned radial engine line up in museums alongside stagecoaches and trolley cars?

Morally, I could not object to either these possibilities or the aeronautical changes that had already taken place in Southeast, for all represented safety improvements. Emotionally, however, I was a sailing ship skipper silently watching a newfangled steamer on the horizon.

If sophistication in aviation had appealed to me, I would have long ago put on the uniform of an airline, commuter, or corporate pilot. But I had chosen blue jeans because romance had felt more comfortable. Now progress threatened to derobe me spiritually. Maybe the Washington, D.C., job opportunity was a timely chance to get out before I became an anachronism, before tomorrow loomed too close. If I waited until the sirens no longer sang, a decent alternate career might be unavailable.

The dilemma seemed to have resolved itself; I'd tell my editor friend to put my name on the masthead. I was unsure whether the sigh that followed came from relief or regret.

The Cessna 206 was at the head of the Endicott River valley now. I banked east slightly to follow it to Lynn Canal. On both sides the valley showed mile after mile of undeveloped forested slopes, rocky bluffs, and meandering streams draining into the river. Here and there a waterfall tumbled down a cliff. Like a visitor leaving a vacation spot, I tried to fix the scene in my memory, certain that I'd never look upon it again.

A movement focused my attention—two animals dashed from the edge of the river into the forest. They were gone in a second, but that was long enough to identify them: wolves! I circled twice, hoping to sight them again. The trees shielded them from me.

As I leveled the wings to continue down the valley, I noticed my vibrating, ghostlike reflection in the side window. The image was smiling back at me in appreciation of the sighting. Despite the blurriness, I detected a sparkle in the eyes. Suddenly, I realized that the smile and the sparkle also represented changes I had experienced. I had seldom had such facial expressions before moving to Alaska. Since then, I had often seen them in my reflection, or felt them in my heart. Long, tough days in the cockpit occasionally erased them, but they always returned, somehow enhanced, like the love between a man and a woman after a spat. When had I ever straightened my tie in front of a mirror in the men's room of an office building and seen a smile or a sparkle? Or felt either inside while working in a newsroom?

I touched my fingers to my forehead in a salute to the wolves. The animals had once again reminded me of the kind of experience that brought joy into my life. They had also reminded me that things change at different rates. Wolves are among nature's most man-shy creatures. A pack might wander near an isolated cabin, but never a community. They were present here because this valley qualified as wilderness. So did many other remote, unspoiled areas of Alaska. By its essence, wilderness could not be developed overnight. As long as Alaska harbored places like this that were wild enough for wolves, it would need old-fashioned bush pilots to fly to them.

Ahead, parts of the canal shimmered in low-angle rays that beamed through saddles and passes in the Chilkat Mountains. Across the canal, a pink hue adorned the snow on the upper slopes of the Coast Mountains. I throttled back to descend.

Blue smoke curling up from a beach at the mouth of the river led my eyes to the mechanic and his wife. They stood by their campfire, waving. As I buzzed by in a greeting, they grinned—grinned not only in their own hello, but also, I knew, to acknowledge a mutual sharing of environment. The mechanic pointed vigorously to the campfire, over which lay a skewered object wrapped in what looked like tinfoil. Apparently the two had caught fish in the river. Maybe they were saving a filet for me.

In a grassy meadow separated from the beach by a stand of trees, I spotted two grizzlies grazing like cattle. Obviously, neither couple was aware of the other; a light breeze placed the bears safely upwind of the campfire, and the trees blocked the humans' view of the meadow. One of the bruins raised its head briefly when my noisy bird flew by, then returned to its feeding.

My spirit melded with the harmony of the evening as I lowered the flaps and lined up for a landing along the beach. Yes, in most ways and places, Alaska was still Alaska. Changes would continue, but I would no longer fret about their direction or impact. What mattered was that I relished my livelihood. In an age of nine-to-five routine, not all people could make that statement. I realized that even the rainy days now seemed less so; I had been around long enough to accept them. At least in retrospect, I could appreciate them for the color and challenges they provided, and for the gusto that developed out of surmounting them.

The time might yet come when Alaskan vignettes like massive glaciers and fleeting wolves would no longer excite me. Someday an office might appeal to me for the lifestyle rather than for security or an image. Meanwhile, the new magazine would have to find someone else, and tomorrow would have to take care of itself. I wasn't through with today.

ABOUT THE AUTHOR

GERRY BRUDER has logged more than 7,000 hours in floatplanes as a commercial pilot in southeastern Alaska and in Seattle. His pilot credentials include an instructor's certificate. As a journalist, he's been a reporter for the Ketchikan *Daily News* and the Anchorage *Times*, a staff writer for *Business & Commercial Aviation* Magazine, an associate editor for *Flying* Magazine, and editor of the *Western Flyer*. Bruder is a native of Connecticut, and he holds degrees from Hanover College and Ohio State University.